This edition published in 1997 by
The Southwestern Company
2451 Atrium Way
Nashville, TN 37214

Reprinted 1998, 2000

LIBRARY OF CONGRESS CATALOGING-IN-PUBLICATION DATA

William, Brian.
The Kingfisher encyclopedia of questions and answers / Brian
Williams.—1st ed.
p.   cm.
Includes index.
Summary: Questions and answers provide information on such topics
as general science, earth and space, the human body, and plants and
animals.
1. Science—Encyclopedias, Juvenile. 2. Science—Miscellanea—
Juvenile literature. [1. Science—Miscellanea. 2. Questions and
answers.] I. Title.
Q121.W55 1997 503—DC21 97-12668 CIP AC

ISBN 0-87197-465-7

Produced by Miles Kelly Publishing Ltd.
Designer: Smiljka Surla
Editors: Rosie Alexander, Kate Miles,
Angela Royston
Assistant Editors: Susanne Bull, Lynne French
Picture Research: Yannick Yago

Printed in Hong Kong / China

Kingfisher

Encyclopedia of
QUESTIONS
and ANSWERS

3

Peoples and Countries
History

SOUTHWESTERN

CONTENTS

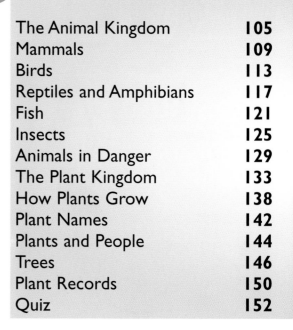

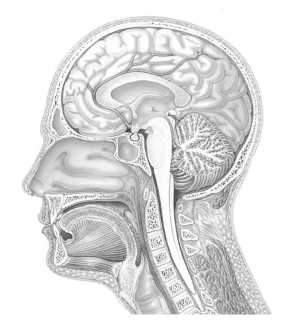

3 PEOPLES AND COUNTRIES

HUMAN BODY

HISTORY

ACKNOWLEDGMENTS

The publishers wish to thank the artists who have contributed toward this book. These include the following:

Susanna Addario; Hemesh Alles; Marion Appleton; Hayward Art Group; Craig Austin; David Barnett; Peter Bull; Vanessa Card; Tony Chance; Kuo Kang Chen; Harry Clow; Stephen Conlin; Peter Dennis; Richard Draper; Eugene Fleury; Chris Forsey; Mark Franklin; Terry Gabbey; Sheila Galbraith; Mark George; Jeremy Gower; Ruby Green; Ray Grinaway; Nick Harris; Nicholas Hewetson; Adam Hook; Christian Hook; Christina Hook; Richard Hook; Tony Kenyon; Mike Lacey; Claire Littlejohn; Mick Loates; Bernard Long; Alan Male; Shane Marsh; Jamie Medlin; Nicki Palin; Alex Pang; Roger Payne; Mel Pickering; Maurice Pledger; Bryan Poole; Sebastian Quigley; Claudia Saraceni; Guy Smith; Tony Smith; Michael Steward; Simon Tegg; Ian Thompson; Ross Watton; Steve Weston; Linda Worrall; David Wright;

Photographs

The publishers wish to thank the following for supplying photographs for this book:

Page 14 (BC) Corbis; 20 (TR) Corbis; 21 (BC) Rich Kirchner/ NHPA; 25 (BR) Corbis; 26 (TR) Corbis; 29 (B) ZEFA; 33 (BC) ZEFA; 34 (BR) David Frazier/ Science Photo Library; 45 (TR) ZEFA; 49 (TR) NHPA; 50 (TR) Corbis; 62 (C) Mehau Kulyk/ Science Photo Library; 65 (CL) Firework Ltd; 68 (T) ZEFA; 71 (TL) Jerome Yeats/ Science Photo Library; 73 (TR) Geoff Tompkinson/ Science Photo Library; 75 (BC) Corbis; 78 (TL) Yves Baulieu/ Publiphoto Diffusion/ Science Photo Library; 81 (TL) Corbis; 96 (CR) Ford; 111 (T) Henry Ausloos/ NHPA; 116 (TL) Bill Coster/ NHPA; 122 (BC) Kevin Cullimore/ Tony Stone Images; 123 (TL) David B. Fleetham/ Oxford Scientific Films; 126 (BR) G.I. Bernard/ Oxford Scientific Films; 131 (B) Hans Reinhard/ Bruce Coleman Ltd.; 136 (C) Georgette/ Douwma/ Planet Earth Pictures; 139 (BL) Stan Osolinski/ Oxford Scientific Films; 142 (BR) Eric Soder/ NHPA; 145 (CR) Alain Compost/ Bruce Coleman Ltd.; 146 (TC) Linda Burgess/ The Garden Picture Library; 146 (C) John Glover/ The Garden Picture Library; 147 (R) Tim Ridley/ Larousse Archives; 149 (TL) E.A. Janes/ NHPA; 149 (CR) Jerry Pavia/ The Garden Picture Library; 150 (TR) Michael Tweddie/ NHPA; 150 (B) David Middleton/ NHPA; 151 (TR) Jerry Pavia/ The Garden Picture Library; 163 (BR) Science Photo Library; 167 (TR) Simon Fraser/ Science Photo Library; 167 (BR) Jeremy Mason/ Science Photo Library; 179 (TL) Will & Deni McIntyre/ Science Photo Library; 182 (BL) Ian West/ Bubbles; 183 (TL) Jeremy Bright/ Robert Harding Picture Library; 183 (BL) Robert Harding; 188 (BL) David Hanson/ Tony Stone Worldwide; 189 (TR) Simon Potter/ Telegraph Colour Library; 189 (BL) Andy Cox/ Tony Stone Images; 191 (TR) AKG Photo; 193 (BL) Donna Day/ Tony Stone Images; 194 (BR) Tony Stone Images; 195 (BR) David Joel/ Tony Stone Worldwide; 198 (BR) F. Rombout/ Bubbles; 199 (TL) St. Bartholomews Hospital/ Science Photo Library; 199 (R) Dave Bartruff/ Corbis; 202 (TL) Peter Lambert/ Tony Stone Worldwide; 202 (BR) The Hutchison Library; 203 (TR) c 1996 Corel Corp.; 204 (TL) c 1996 Corel Corp.; 204 (TR) Christine Osborne Pictures; 206 (BR) Jean-Leo Dugust/ Panos Pictures; 207 (BL) Carla Signorini Jones/ Images of Africa Photobank; 207 (BR) Jeremy A. Horner/ The Hutchison Library; 209 (TL) Hugh Sitton/ Tony Stone Images; 209 (BR) Spectrum Colour Library; 210 (TL) Oldrich Karasck/ Tony Stone Images; 212 (CL) Paul Harris/ Tony Stone Images; 212 (BR) c 1996 Corel Corp.; 213 (TL) Alain le Garsmeur/ Panos Pictures; 214 (BC) Paul Chesley/ Tony Stone Worldwide; 215 (TR) c 1996 Corel Corp.; 216/7 (CR) Spectrum Colour Library; 218 (TL) ZEFA; 218 (BL) Spectrum Colour Library; 219 (CR) Spectrum Colour Library; 222 (BL) Rohan/ Tony Stone Images; 223 (TL) ZEFA; 225 (TR) ZEFA; 225 (BR) D. Saunders/ Trip; 228 (CR) c 1996 Corel Corp.; 231 (TR) ZEFA; 231 (BL) Jaemsen/ ZEFA; 232 (BR) Spectrum Colour Library; 235 (C) ZEFA; 237 (CR) Spectrum Colour Library; 238 (BR) The Hutchison Library; 238 (BL) ZEFA; 239 (BR) Paul Chesley/ Tony Stone Worldwide; 239 (BL) Jeff Britnell/ Tony Stone; 241 (TR) Luc Delahaye/ Sipa Press/ Rex Features; 242 (TC) Sipa Press/ Rex Features; 242 (BR) John Lamb/ Tony Stone Images; 242 (BL) Persuy/ Sipa Press/ Rex Features; 243 (TL) Spectrum Colour Library; 245 (BL) Images Colour Library; 245 (CR) Marian Morrison/ South American Pictures; 246 (CL) Eric Lawne/ The Hutchison Library; 247 (TL) Robert Harding Picture Library; 247 (BR) Jon Burbank/ The Hutchison Library; 254 (CR) Andrew Hill/ The Hutchison Library; 260 (C) Palais de Versailles, Musee Historique AKG Photo; 260 (BR) Peter Newark's Historical Pictures; 261 (TL) Peter Newark's American Pictures; 261 (C) Popperfoto; 261 (BC) Popperfoto; 266 (TR) The Hulton Getty Picture Collection Ltd.; 268 (CR) Corbis; 271 (BR) Simon Krectmem/ Reuter Popperfoto; 275 (BL) AKG Photo; 278 (CT) E.T. Archive; 278 (B) AKG Photo; 279 (CT) AKG Photo; 279 (BL) E.T. Archive; 279 (BR) Popperfoto; 281 (TL) The Hulton Getty Picture Collection Ltd.; 281 (BL) Mary Evans Picture Library; 281 (BR) AKG Photo; 282 (BR) Mary Evans Picture Library; 282 (CL) Disney Video; 283 (TC) The Bettman Archive/ Corbis; 284 (BR) Ancient Art & Architecture Collection Ltd.; 285 (BR) Leipzig Museum/ AKG Photo; 286 (CT) Peter Newark's American Pictures; 286 (BR) Corbis; 286 (CL) Peter Newark's American Pictures; 288 (CL) Steve Etherington/ EMPICS; 288 (BR) Mike Blake/ Reuters Popperfoto; 289 (TL) The Times/ Rex Features; 289 (BR) Popperfoto; 293 (TL) Nelson Museum, Monmouth; E.T Archive 293 (R) AKG Photo London; 294 (BL) BFI Stills, Posters & Designs; 295 (TL) Peter Newark's American Pictures; 295 (BC) Peter Newark's American Pictures.

AFRICA

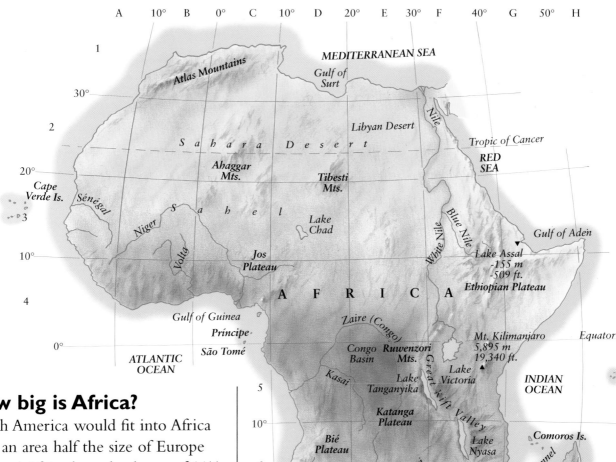

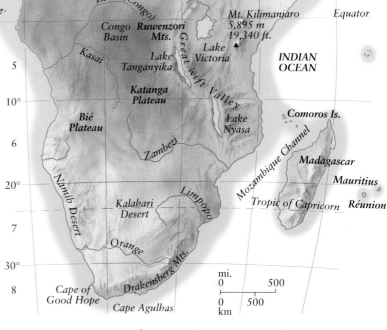

How big is Africa?

North America would fit into Africa with an area half the size of Europe to spare! Africa has a land area of 11½ million square miles (30 million sq km). It is more than 5,000 miles (8,000 km) long from north to south, and more than 3,700 miles (6,000 km) wide from east to west.

Africa is mostly a huge jungle: true or false?

False. Most of Africa is either desert (40 percent) or grassy savannah (40 percent). Forests cover less than a fifth of Africa.

Where are the Mountains of the Moon?

The Ruwenzori Mountains are on the border between Uganda and

▲ The map of Africa shows how much of the continent is desert. There are also large expanses of grassland. The rain forests are in central and western Africa.

Zaire (Dem. Rep. of Congo) in central Africa. These peaks are over 16,400 feet (5,000 m) high. They were named the Mountains of the Moon by the early geographer Ptolemy, who in A.D. 150 drew a map showing the Nile River that began in these mountains. The river has several sources, including Lake Victoria.

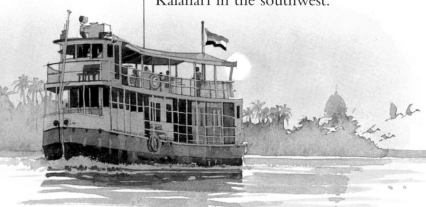

◀ **Tourists walk along the crest of a huge sand dune in Namibia. The Namib is one of Africa's driest deserts.**

Is there much desert in Africa?

About 40 percent of Africa is desert. The Sahara Desert covers much of the northern third of the continent. Other deserts are the Namib and the Kalahari in the southwest.

What is the Great Rift Valley?

The Great Rift Valley is one of Africa's outstanding natural features: a series of valleys that cuts through eastern Africa. The Great Rift Valley is the result of enormous volcanic movement. In places, the rift in the Earth is over 1 mile (1.5 km) deep and 25 miles (40 km) wide. In other places, the rift has filled with water, creating some of Africa's greatest lakes (Mobutu Sese Seko, Edward, Nyasa, and Tanganyika), as well as the Red Sea.

How high is the land in Africa?

Compared to Asia or North America, Africa is fairly flat. The north, west, and center of the continent are mostly less than 2,000 feet (600 m) above sea level. Most of northern Africa is the plateau of the Sahara. The highest land is in the east and south. This area includes the Great Rift Valley and the grassy plains of the Eastern Highlands.

▲ **Boats carry goods and passengers along the Nile River. This mighty river is the lifeblood of Egypt, and has been for thousands of years.**

Like all rivers, the Nile is hard to measure because its course constantly changes. It is about 4,150 miles (6,670 km) long.

▶ **Tugela River tumbles over a series of falls, creating a spectacular, natural wonder.**

Which are Africa's greatest rivers?

Africa's biggest rivers are the Nile (the longest river in the world), followed by the Zaire (Congo), the Niger, and the Zambezi.

Where is Tugela Falls?

Tugela Falls is a series of five waterfalls on the Tugela River in South Africa. The highest fall is 1,350 feet (410 m) high and the total drop is 3,106 feet (950 m). Tugela is the second highest waterfall in the world.

Is there any snow in Africa?

Africa's highest mountain is in Tanzania in eastern Africa. It is Kilimanjaro or Uhuru ("Freedom") and is 19,340 feet (5,895 m) high. Kilimanjaro is an extinct volcano. Although very near the Equator, the summit is always covered with snow.

Which is Africa's largest island?

The island of Madagascar, off the eastern coast of Africa, covers 226,640 square miles. It is the fourth biggest island in the world and is separated from the mainland by the Mozambique Channel. Madagascar has animals found nowhere else in the world, such as lemurs and rare birds. Most of its people rely on agriculture.

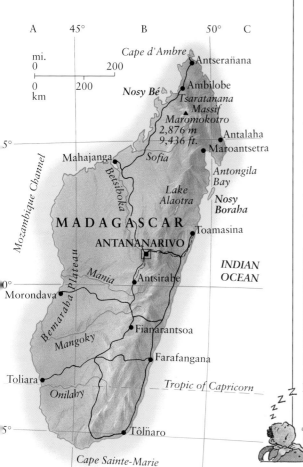

▲ **Kilimanjaro's snowcapped peak can be seen from far away. The mountain towers above the vast plains where elephants and many other animals roam.**

◀ **Central Madagascar is a high plateau. There are lowlands in the east and south. Many of the island's natural forests have been cut down.**

On the island of Madagascar, a man makes a speech to his bride-to-be before she will marry him. If the speech is no good, he pays a fine and starts all over again!

When did people first live in Africa?

Africa is where human beings are first thought to have evolved. Scientists have found bones and other remains of humanlike creatures that are older than remains found elsewhere. These creatures lived more than 4 million years ago. About 2 million years ago the first true humans lived in Africa, hunting animals, gathering plants, and making the first stone tools. These people are known as *Homo habilis* ("skillful human").

▼ **The humanlike creature *Australopithecus* lived in Africa over 4 million years ago, and may have used sticks and stones as tools.**

What is the "smoke that thunders?"

Near the Zambia–Zimbabwe border the Zambezi River plunges over the Victoria Falls. This is Africa's most spectacular waterfall, 350 feet (108 m) high and 1 mile (1.5 km) wide. As the river pours over the falls, a great mist of spray rises into the air and the thunder of the water can be heard far away. The African name for the falls is *Mosi-oa-tunya*, which means "the smoke that thunders."

Why is drought a problem in Africa?

Rainfall in Africa is very uneven. Some parts of the continent, such as the western rain forests, get rain all year round. Drier areas may go for years without a shower. Much of Africa has one or two wet seasons each year. If these rains fail, crops do not grow and people starve. Drought

◀ **The Victoria Falls are one of the most impressive sights in the world. Clouds of spray are thrown up by the water crashing down into the gorge below.**

▶ **Lack of water is a big problem in several countries of Africa, such as Ethiopia. Nomadic people often carry water with them.**

In the Sahara, sand blown by the driving wind can strip paint off a car—like a giant sheet of sandpaper. Camels need their tough skins!

(lack of rain) has been a cause of famine in the lands fringing the Sahara and in Ethiopia in northeast Africa.

What is the harmattan?

The harmattan is an African wind. It blows from the Sahara westward and southwestward from December to February. The harmattan is dry and also cool, because the desert is cooler at this time of year. It carries dust from the Sahara across neighboring countries.

Why is Africa a warm continent?

The Equator runs across the middle of Africa, and all but a tenth of Africa is within the tropics. Temperatures are high all year round, and there is little difference between summer and winter. The Sahara in the north is one of the hottest places in the world.

Which is Africa's largest country?

The biggest country in Africa is the Sudan. It has an area of nearly 1 million square miles (2.5 million sq km). The north is bleak desert, but in the south are grassy plains. The Nile River creates a big marshy area, the Sudd.

How do Bushmen survive in the desert?

The Bushmen, or San, are people of southwest Africa. A few still roam the Kalahari Desert, where there is little water and few trees. The Bushmen are skillful hunters and trackers and gather foods such as insects, roots, and berries. They can find drinking water underground in roots and wet sand. They can live in a land so harsh that outsiders would soon die of thirst and hunger. Like many Africans, the Bushmen are now giving up their traditional ways.

Which African men wear veils?

The Tuareg are nomads of northern Africa. They roam in or around the Sahara Desert. The Tuareg are Berbers, a people who lived here long before Arabs settled northern

AFRICA FACTS

■ Area: 11,704,000 sq. mi. (30,313,000 sq km).

■ Population: about 750 million people.

■ Number of countries: 53.

■ Longest river: Nile 4,150 miles (6,670 km).

■ Largest lake: Lake Victoria 26,828 sq. mi.

■ Highest mountain: Mt. Kilimanjaro 19,340 feet (5,900 m).

■ Largest country: Sudan.

■ Country with most people: Nigeria.

■ Largest city: Cairo.

■ The oldest nation in Africa is Ethiopia, which has been independent for about 2,000 years.

▼ Desert nomads like the Tuareg wander from place to place with their animals. They know where to find food and water.

Africa. They are Muslims, but it is the Tuareg men, not the women, who hide their faces behind veils. Once the Tuareg raided and traded across the Sahara, but most have now abandoned their old desert life.

How do Africa's nomads live?

Some Africans still follow traditional ways of living like the nomads of the Sahara region and northeast Africa. These people wander with herds of camels, sheep, and goats. They have no settled homes but keep moving in search of fresh pasture for their animals.

Was the Sahara once green?

About 10,000 years ago, the Sahara was much wetter than it is now. Where there are now only rocks and sand, there were lakes and streams. Trees and grass were able to grow, and animals such as elephants, giraffes, and antelope were plentiful. About 6,000 years ago the climate began to change and the Sahara became drier. People and animals were forced to move away as green land began to turn into desert. The Sahara is still spreading.

◄ Benin is famous for its art, such as these bronze figures of a king and two kneeling subjects. African artists have influenced the ideas of modern Western artists, such as Picasso.

In which African country, besides Egypt, can you see pyramids?

The Sudan is a huge, dry country in northeast Africa. At Meroë, east of Khartoum, you can see the ruins of pyramids built more than 2,000 years ago. Between 592 B.C. and A.D. 350 Meroë was a powerful kingdom. The people of Meroë worshiped the gods of Ancient Egypt.

Where did Benin people live?

The Benin people lived in West Africa, south of the Niger River. Four hundred years ago, they made beautiful objects out of ivory, wood, and bronze. From about A.D. 1000, powerful African states such as Benin, Kanem–Borno, and Songhai ruled large territories in West Africa.

Which northern African country is famous for leather goods?

Morocco in northern Africa. Ancient cities such as Fez and Marrakesh have tanneries where goat skins are treated and dyed to make leather. Most Moroccans are poor and own small plots of land on which they graze sheep, cattle, and goats. Morocco is an ancient Islamic kingdom and most of its people are Arabs, but about a third are Berbers. Morocco has been ruled by the kings of the Alawi dynasty since the 1600s.

▲ These ruined pyramids are at Meroë, east of Khartoum in the Sudan. The people of Meroë would have seen and admired the pyramids of Egypt, to the north.

◄ At a Moroccan tannery, workers soak and treat animal skins to turn them into leather. Tanning is a messy and smelly business!

Which countries share the Kariba Dam?

This hydroelectric scheme was completed in 1959 with the building of a dam across the Zambezi River. The dam provides power for Zambia's copper industry and also for Zimbabwe. The damming of the Zambezi created an artificial lake, Lake Kariba.

Where is Table Mountain?

Table Mountain is South Africa's most famous landmark. For many visitors, the first sight of South Africa is the city of Cape Town, beneath the backdrop of Table Mountain.

Where can you visit a gold mine beneath a city?

In Johannesburg, South Africa. The city began in the gold boom of the late 1800s, and is now a center of commerce. Visitors can explore a gold mine beneath the city and a museum showing life in the gold rush.

▼ **A view of Cape Town from Signal Hill. In the background rises Table Mountain. Visitors can ride the cableway to the top.**

▶ **The Kariba Dam was built to provide a source of energy for both Zambia and Zimbabwe. Behind the dam is Lake Kariba.**

AFRICA'S WEALTH

- Africa exports petroleum, gold, and diamonds, and other minerals, such as cobalt.

- South Africa is the world's largest producer of gold.

- Crops grown in Africa include corn, cocoa, cassava, palm kernels, vanilla beans, yams, bananas, coffee, cotton, rubber, sugar, and tea.

- Africans raise two-thirds of the world's camels!

- Africans raise a third of the world's goats. They also keep cattle and sheep in large numbers.

- Africa has about a quarter of the world's forests.

- About 40 percent of Africa's factory-made goods are made in South Africa.

Which is the biggest city in Africa?

Cairo, the capital of Egypt, is the biggest city in Africa. It is a bustling, dusty city full of hooting taxis and hurrying crowds. Modern hotels and office blocks rise up next to old mosques and basic housing where the city's poor people live. About 9.7 million people live in Cairo.

▲ **Cairo, Africa's largest city, has grown at a rapid pace in modern times, with many new buildings. These provide an interesting contrast with the traditional bazaars and cafés.**

ASIA

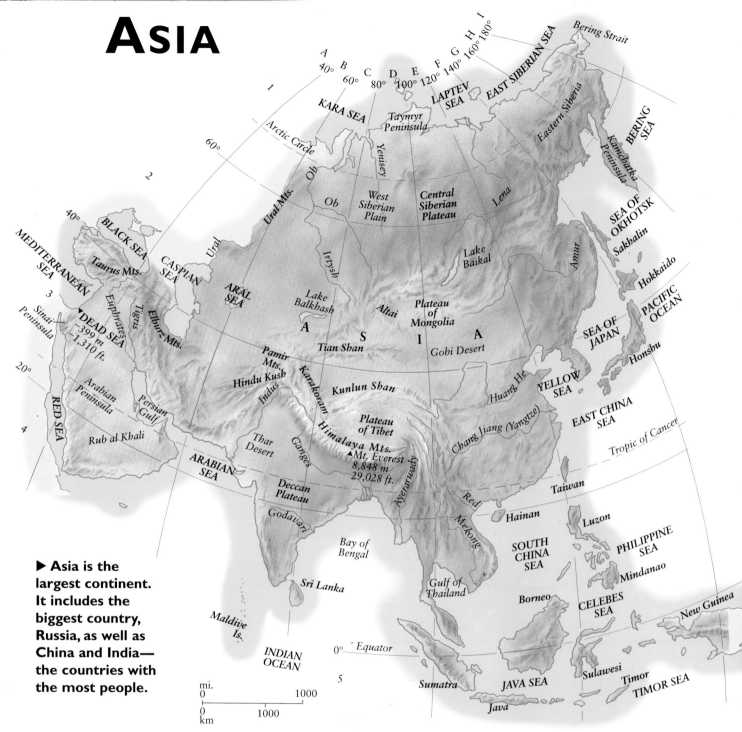

A
40°
B
60°
C
80°
D
100°
E
F
120°
G
140°
H
160°
I
180°

1

2

3

4

5

Bering Strait

KARA SEA

Arctic Circle

60°

Taymyr Peninsula

LAPTEV SEA

EAST SIBERIAN SEA

Eastern Siberia

BERING SEA

Kamchatka Peninsula

Yenisey

Ob

West Siberian Plain

Central Siberian Plateau

Lena

SEA OF OKHOTSK

Sakhalin

Amur

Hokkaido

MEDITERRANEAN SEA

40°

BLACK SEA

CASPIAN SEA

Taurus Mts.

Ural Mts.

Ob

Irtysh

Lake Baikal

PACIFIC OCEAN

Sinai Peninsula

Euphrates

Tigris

Elburz Mts.

ARAL SEA

Lake Balkhash

Altai

Plateau of Mongolia

A   S   I   A

SEA OF JAPAN

Honshu

▼DEAD SEA
−399 m
−1,310 ft.

20°

Pamir Mts.

Tian Shan

Gobi Desert

Huang He

YELLOW SEA

Arabian Peninsula

Persian Gulf

Hindu Kush

Indus

Karakoram

Kunlun Shan

Chang Jiang (Yangtze)

EAST CHINA SEA

RED SEA

Plateau of Tibet

Tropic of Cancer

Rub al Khali

Thar Desert

Ganges

Himalaya Mts.

▲Mt. Everest
8,848 m
29,028 ft.

Ayeyarwady

Red

Taiwan

ARABIAN SEA

Deccan Plateau

Godavari

Mekong

Hainan

Luzon

Sri Lanka

Bay of Bengal

SOUTH CHINA SEA

PHILIPPINE SEA

Mindanao

▶ **Asia is the largest continent. It includes the biggest country, Russia, as well as China and India— the countries with the most people.**

Maldive Is.

INDIAN OCEAN

0°   *Equator*

Borneo

CELEBES SEA

New Guinea

Sulawesi

Timor

TIMOR SEA

mi.
0   1000
0   1000
km

Sumatra

JAVA SEA

Java

How big is Asia?

Asia is the biggest continent. Its area of 17 million square miles (44 million sq km) is greater than North and South America put together, and four times greater than Europe. The coastline of Asia is almost 81,000 miles (130,000 km) long—more than three times the distance around the world.

Some mountains get smaller all the time as they are worn away. The Himalayas are getting higher, pushed up by movements in the Earth's crust.

What are Asia's main features?

Asia's natural features are very varied, from the world's highest mountains (the Himalayas) to long rivers (such as the Chang Jiang), lakes as big as seas (the Caspian), and deserts like the Gobi. There are hot jungles, cold forests, grasslands, and snowy tundras.

Which country has the most languages?

India has 14 major languages and more than 160 others. There are also 700 dialects (local or regional variations). Hindi is the official language of India, and many Indians also speak English.

Where is the Khyber Pass?

The Khyber Pass is in northwest Pakistan. Here the land is rugged and hilly. The pass is a route through the mountains to Afghanistan.

What is the Tonlé Sap?

The Tonlé Sap is a large lake in Cambodia, in Southeast Asia. During the summer floods, its waters cover 3,900 square miles (10,000 sq km). The lake is formed by water from the Mekong River, the longest river in Southeast Asia (2,800 miles) and the fifth longest in Asia.

Where are Asia's high and low points?

Asia has the highest and lowest points on the Earth's land. Mount Everest (over 28,000 [8,800 km] feet above sea level) is the highest point. The shores of the Dead Sea (about 1,310 feet [400m] below sea level) are the lowest points to be found anywhere on land.

Where are Asia's deepest gorges?

The deepest gorges cut by rivers are those made by the Indus, Brahmaputra, and Ganges, which flow through India and Pakistan. In places, these rivers cut gorges that are more than 3 miles (5 km) deep.

Does Asia have more people than any other continent?

Yes. Besides covering one third of the Earth's land surface, Asia has about three-fifths of the world's people. More than 3.5 billion people live in Asia, in 49 countries.

▲ In the Dead Sea, you can float while reading the paper! This is because the water is unusually salty and supports your weight.

ASIA FACTS

- Area: 17,135,000 sq. mi. (44,380,000 sq km).
- Population 3.5 billion.
- Number of countries: 49.
- Longest river: Chang Jiang (Yangtze), 3,900 miles (6,300 km).
- Largest lake: Caspian Sea, 144,000 sq. mi. (372,000 sq km).
- Highest mountain: Everest 29,000 feet.
- Largest country: Russia (partly in Europe).
- Country with most people: China.
- Largest city: Tokyo, over 26 million people.

▼ The Tonlé Sap is a large lake in Cambodia. People in this region use the rivers and the lakes for transportation and fishing.

Which is the highest mountain in India?

To the north of India rise the mighty Himalayas, the highest mountains in the world. The highest peaks, including Mount Everest itself, are in Nepal, but India, too, has some towering peaks. The highest mountain in India is Nanda Devi, which is 25,410 feet (7,817 m) high.

Where is the Roof of the World?

The Roof of the World is the name given to a region north of India where several mighty mountain ranges meet. Here are the highest mountains on Earth, including the peaks of the Himalayas, the Tien Shan, the Kunlun Shan, the Karakoram, and the Pamirs.

In which country do people live longest?

Every country has a few people who live to an exceptionally great age—100 or more. In Japan the average life expectancy (the age a newborn baby can expect to live) is 77. This is higher than

◀ **Climbers from all over the world come to the Himalaya Mountains to climb Mount Everest and the other peaks.**

Some people also call Tibet the Roof of the World because it is so high and remote. Tibet was once a free country but is now controlled by China.

in Europe or the United States. In some poor countries of Africa the life expectancy is only 45 to 50.

How many islands make up Japan?

Japan is a bow-shaped chain of islands which stretches for about 1,200 miles (1,900 km). There are four main islands, called Honshu (the biggest), Hokkaido, Shikoku, and Kyushu. There are about 3,000 smaller islands.

Which is Japan's most famous mountain?

Japan has more than 160 volcanoes, about a third of which are active. The most famous is Fujiyama, or Mount Fuji. It is the highest mountain in

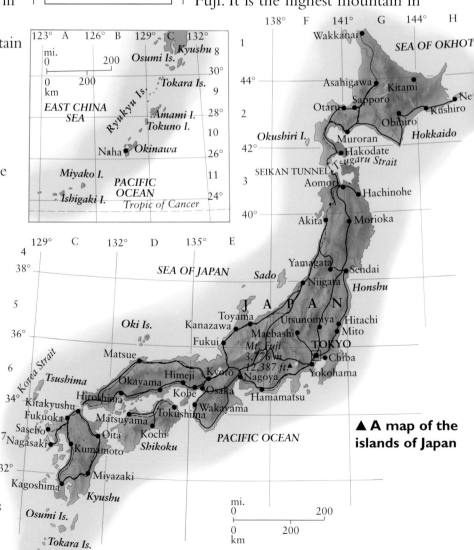

▲ **A map of the islands of Japan**

Japan (12,400 feet [3,780 m]). This cone-shaped volcano last erupted in 1707. To the people of Japan, Fujiyama is a sacred mountain. Every year thousands climb to the top of the mountain, as a spiritual pilgrimage.

What are the Maldives?

The Maldives are a chain of low-lying coral islands in the Indian Ocean. Some of the islands belong to India. The rest make up the republic of the Maldives, a separate country. There are more than 2,000 islands, but fewer than 200 are big enough for people to live on.

Where is Angkor Wat?

Angkor Wat is a temple in Cambodia and the biggest religious building in the world. It was built by the Khmer people of Southeast Asia in the 1100s in honor of a Hindu god. Later Buddhists added to the temple buildings. Angkor Wat was abandoned by the 1500s. Wooden buildings rotted away and the stone temple was overgrown by forest. In the 1860s a Frenchman discovered the ruins.

▲ **Mount Fuji is crowned with snow, which melts in summer. The top of the mountain is often hidden by clouds.**

DID YOU KNOW?

■ The smallest Asian nations are tiny, like Bahrain which covers only 240 sq. mi. (622 sq km).

■ Although China has more than a billion people, most of the country is deserts or mountains with very few people.

■ All the world's major religions—Judaism, Christianity, Islam, Hinduism, and Buddhism —began in Asia.

■ Asians speak many languages. In India alone, there are hundreds of local dialects.

■ The most prosperous countries of Asia include oil-rich Saudi Arabia and manufacturing giants such as Japan, Korea, Taiwan, and Singapore.

■ Indonesia has 13,000 islands, more than any island group in the world.

▼ **The Maldives are a string of coral reef islands in the Indian Ocean, south of the Indian subcontinent. Only the larger ones are shown here.**

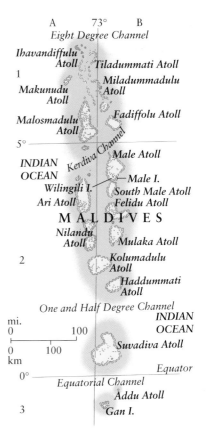

A 73° B
Eight Degree Channel

Ihavandiffulu Atoll
1
Makunudu Atoll
Malosmadulu Atoll

Tiladummati Atoll
Miladummadulu Atoll
Fadiffolu Atoll

5°

INDIAN OCEAN
Kerdiva Channel
Wilingili I.
Ari Atoll

Male Atoll
Male I.
South Male Atoll
Felidu Atoll

M A L D I V E S

Nilandu Atoll
2

Mulaka Atoll
Kolumadulu Atoll
Haddummati Atoll

One and Half Degree Channel
mi.
0   100
0   100
km

INDIAN OCEAN

Suvadiva Atoll

0°
Equatorial Channel

Equator

Addu Atoll
3
Gan I.

Where is Siberia?

East of the Ural Mountains lies Siberia, a wilderness of 5½ million square miles (14 million sq km) stretching to the Pacific Ocean. Siberia is a region of vast forests, rivers, and frozen plains. Here are the coldest inhabited places in the world; winter temperatures drop to −42°F (−67°C).

▼ Traveling by reindeer sled is a good way to get around in Kamchatka, Siberia, where winters are long and cold.

Which is Asia's longest river?

The Chang Jiang, or Yangtze Kiang, in China is the longest river in Asia. It flows into the South China Sea.

Which Asian city is sacred to three religions?

Jerusalem is a holy city for people of three faiths: Jews, Christians, and Muslims. Jerusalem was divided between Israel and Jordan until 1967. Since then Israel has held all of the city. For Jews, Jerusalem is the ancient Hebrew capital, where King Solomon built the Temple. For Christians, the city is where Jesus Christ preached and was crucified. Muslims believe that Muhammad rose to heaven from a rock in Jerusalem.

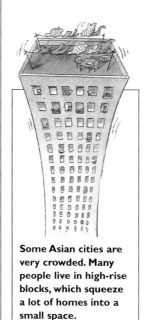

Some Asian cities are very crowded. Many people live in high-rise blocks, which squeeze a lot of homes into a small space.

Which rivers are known as the "cradle of civilization?"

Ancient civilizations grew up near rivers. Rivers were trade routes and provided water for farming. Several great civilizations arose in Asia. The rivers Tigris and Euphrates in Mesopotamia (now Iraq) gave rise to the civilizations of Sumer and Babylon over 5,000 years ago. The Indus river valley in Pakistan was the center of another great ancient civilization, known for its cities.

Where is Asia's biggest island?

The island of Borneo is the biggest island in Asia. Its 284,200 square miles (736,000 sq km) are shared by three countries: Malaysia, Indonesia, and Brunei. Borneo is a mountainous island, and much of it is covered in dense rain forest, although logging companies are steadily cutting down the trees for timber.

▲ The Dome of the Rock in Jerusalem is a Muslim shrine, or holy place. The city is sacred to Muslims, Christians, and Jews.

◀ Dubai is one of the oil-rich United Arab Emirates. In this shop, people can buy gold.

The world's biggest gas station is in Jeddah, Saudi Arabia. It has more than 200 pumps!

Where are Asia's richest countries?

A country's wealth is measured in different ways. One way is to work out the average wealth per person (supposing that all the country's wealth could be divided equally between all its people). The oil–producing countries of the Middle East, such as the United Arab Emirates, have small populations, but enormous national wealth from selling oil.

Which is the only city situated on two continents?

Istanbul in Turkey lies in Europe and Asia. It is built on both banks of the Bosporus, the strait that separates these two continents, and is sometimes called the "Gateway to Asia." This great city has had three names. Founded by the Ancient Greeks, it was first called Byzantium, but was renamed Constantinople by the Romans in A.D. 330. In 1453 the Turks captured the city and it became known as Istanbul. It is the largest city in modern Turkey.

Why is Bahrain a true desert island?

The island of Bahrain in the Persian Gulf has hardly any rain. For several months of the year no clouds are seen, and the average annual rainfall is less than 4 inches (100 mm). Despite being mostly desert, Bahrain is rich, because it sells oil abroad.

What is it like learning to write Chinese?

In China, and in Japan too, writing can be an art. People sometimes write words slowly and beautifully using a brush instead of a pen. About 50,000 symbols can be used to write Chinese. Fortunately, children only have to learn about 5,000 of them.

▼ Japanese children learn calligraphy— writing with a brush and ink.

Where is the longest wall on Earth?

The Great Wall of China is the longest structure ever built. It is about 1,500 miles (2,400 km) long and was built in about 210 B.C. to keep out invaders on China's northern borders.

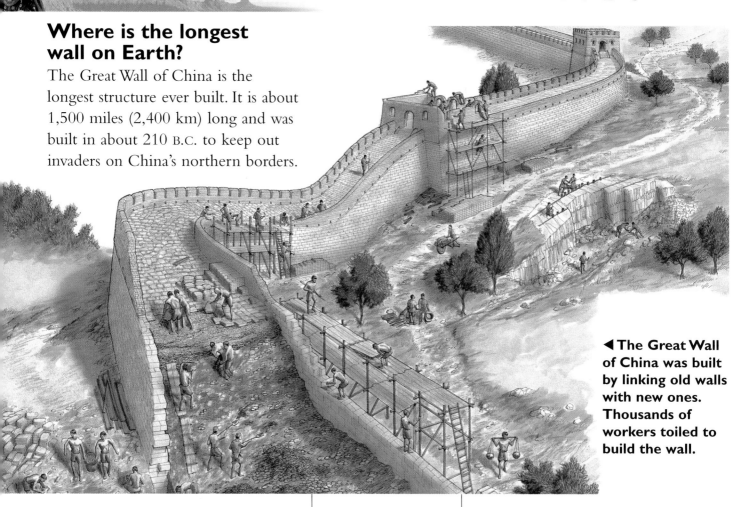

◀ The Great Wall of China was built by linking old walls with new ones. Thousands of workers toiled to build the wall.

Which city has the most crowded commuter trains?

Japan has a highly efficient rail system including high-speed electric trains and the world's longest rail tunnel, the Seikan Tunnel (34 miles [54 km] long). People going to work in Tokyo cram into the city's commuter trains. Trains can be so crowded that railroad staff, called crushers, push in the passengers while the doors close. Tokyo is huge, and people travel from suburbs to work in offices, shops, and factories.

▼ In Tokyo, Japan, station staff push commuters onto crowded trains during the rush hour.

When did North Korea become a communist state?

North Korea is a communist country where all factories and farms, and even cars, are owned by the government. North and South Korea formed a single country from the 1300s until 1910, when Japan occupied Korea. This occupation ended in 1945 when Japan was defeated in World War II. After this the country was divided, and in 1948 North Korea became a communist state. Ever since the Korean War (1950–1953), there have been tensions between North and South Korea. South Korea has a free-market economy, and many people earn high wages in factories.

What is Buddha Park?

Buddha Park lies about 12 miles (20 km) from Vientiane, the capital of Laos. It is a site built in the 1950s to honor the Buddhist and Hindu religions, and the park contains Hindu and Buddhist sculptures. Many people in Laos are Buddhists, although during the 1970s the country had a communist government.

Where are the ruins of Mohenjo-Daro?

In Pakistan. Mohenjo-Daro was an important center of the Indus valley civilization which flourished about 4,000 years ago. It was one of the earliest examples of a planned city, with streets laid out to a grid pattern and good drains.

Where do people live in stilt houses?

Many island people in Indonesia and the Philippines live on boats or in wooden houses built on stilts over the water. The Philippines has over 7,000 tropical islands. Indonesia has more than 13,000!

◄ **Buddha Park in Laos is famous for its statues. The park is near the country's capital, Vientiane.**

▶ **Many people think the Taj Mahal is the most beautiful building in the world. Tourists from many countries come to see it.**

MORE FACTS ON ASIA

■ People in Japan, as well as China, eat with chopsticks.

■ The most popular sport in Japan is baseball.

■ In some Asian cities, you can ride in a pedicab—a taxicab pulled by a driver riding a bicycle.

■ Indian music sounds different from that of the West because it uses a different scale.

■ In Bali, dancers tell stories without words, relying on movements.

■ Among Asia's rarest animals are the giant panda, snow leopard, and Indian rhinoceros.

Where is the Taj Mahal?

This beautiful tomb stands in a garden outside the city of Agra in India. The Mogul Emperor Shah Jahan had the Taj Mahal built in memory of his favorite wife, Mumtaz Mahal. It was built from the 1630s to the 1650s.

Why do people bathe in the Ganges River?

Hindus from all over India come to the Ganges River to bathe in its waters. They visit the holy city of Varanasi, to worship in the city's 1,500 temples and wade into the Ganges at bathing places called ghats.

Where is Singapore?

Singapore is a tiny island country in Southeast Asia. The name means "city of the lions." The city of Singapore has grown from a small fishing village in the 1820s to become one of Asia's chief trading and banking centers.

Which is the biggest city in Asia?

Tokyo in Japan has grown so large that it and nearby Yokohama, now form a huge metropolis of more than 26 million people.

NORTH AND CENTRAL AMERICA

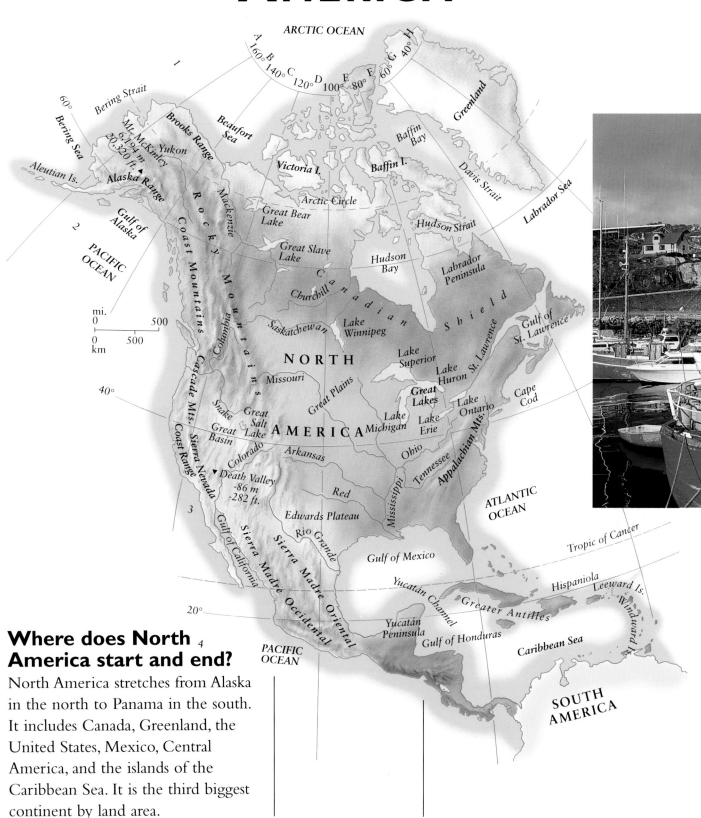

ARCTIC OCEAN

A 160° B 140° C 120° D 100° E 80° F 60° G 40° H

Bering Strait

Beaufort Sea

Baffin Bay

Greenland

Bering Sea

Brooks Range

Mt. McKinley 6,194 m 20,320 ft.

Yukon

Alaska Range

Victoria I.

Baffin I.

Davis Strait

Aleutian Is.

Gulf of Alaska

Coast Mountains

Mackenzie

Arctic Circle

Great Bear Lake

Hudson Strait

Labrador Sea

PACIFIC OCEAN

Rocky Mountains

Great Slave Lake

Hudson Bay

Labrador Peninsula

Churchill

Canadian Shield

Gulf of St. Lawrence

mi. 0   500

0   500 km

Columbia

Saskatchewan

Lake Winnipeg

NORTH

Lake Superior

St. Lawrence

Cascade Mts.

Missouri

Great Plains

Lake Huron

Great Lakes

Cape Cod

40°

Snake

Great Salt Lake

AMERICA

Lake Michigan

Lake Ontario

Lake Erie

Sierra Nevada

Great Basin

Colorado

Arkansas

Ohio

Tennessee

Appalachian Mts.

Coast Range

Death Valley -86 m -282 ft.

Red

Mississippi

ATLANTIC OCEAN

3

Edwards Plateau

Gulf of California

Rio Grande

Tropic of Cancer

Sierra Madre Oriental

Gulf of Mexico

Yucatán Channel

Hispaniola

Leeward Is.

Greater Antilles

Windward Is.

20°

Yucatán Peninsula

Gulf of Honduras

Caribbean Sea

4

PACIFIC OCEAN

SOUTH AMERICA

Where does North America start and end?

North America stretches from Alaska in the north to Panama in the south. It includes Canada, Greenland, the United States, Mexico, Central America, and the islands of the Caribbean Sea. It is the third biggest continent by land area.

Which is North America's largest country?

Canada at more than 3,849,000 square miles (9,970,000 sq km). The United States is smaller, covering 3,619,000 square miles (9,373,000 sq km). Yet only 29 million people live in Canada compared to over 268 million in the United States.

Mexico City's population is growing rapidly. The United Nations calculates that by the year 2000, Mexico City will have more than 19 million people.

◄ **Julianehaab is a port in southern Greenland. Ice covers 80 percent of this northern island.**

▼ **This map shows the different climate regions of North America, from the Arctic north to the tropical south.**

Is Greenland part of North America?

Greenland is a self-governing part of Denmark, a country in Europe. Yet geographically this enormous island is part of North America.

Which is North America's biggest city?

Mexico City, with over 16.5 million people, is the biggest city in North America. The largest city in the United States is New York, with a population of 16 million.

Which is North America's smallest country?

Of the 23 independent North American countries the smallest is St. Kitts and Nevis, an island state in the Caribbean. The islands have a combined area of 104 square miles (269 sq km) and only 44,000 people live there. There are even smaller island states in the region, but they are not self-governing.

What is the climate of North America like?

North America has every kind of climate. The far north is ice-covered all year round. The interior has mostly cold winters and either warm or mild summers. The southeast is warm and moist. The southwest is mostly dry with great ranges of temperature and areas of desert. In the far south, in Central America, there are hot, wet tropical forests.

Climate Regions of North America

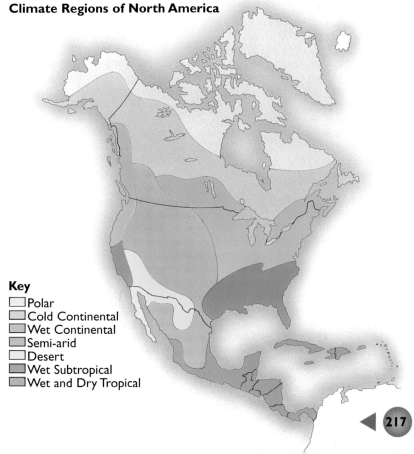

Key
- Polar
- Cold Continental
- Wet Continental
- Semi-arid
- Desert
- Wet Subtropical
- Wet and Dry Tropical

Which is North America's hottest spot?

The highest temperature ever recorded in North America was 135°F (57°C) at Death Valley in California, in 1913.

Where is Yosemite Falls?

Yosemite Falls, the highest waterfall in North America at 2,420 feet (740 m), is in Yosemite National Park, California.

▲ **Pioneers found Death Valley difficult to cross because of the heat and lack of water.**

▶ **Visitors to the Everglades can take a boat trip to watch alligators and other wild animals.**

◀ **Yosemite Falls in California, where a mountain creek falls in three stages, linked by a cascade.**

Where is the world's longest frontier?

The boundary between Canada and the United States stretches for 4,000 miles (6,400 km)—the longest in the world. The border was established in the 1800s, when the newly independent United States was expanding across the western territories and Canada was still governed by Britain. Today, the two nations are friendly neighbors and share much in common. Canadians are greatly outnumbered by Americans.

What are badlands?

Badlands are areas of steep hills and gullies cut by rushing streams. Soil is thin, and few plants can grow there. The climate is usually dry. Sudden heavy rainstorms cause floods which wash away soil and wear the rocks. The Badlands National Park in South Dakota has a spectacular rocky landscape.

What are the Everglades?

The Everglades are subtropical swamps in the south of Florida. The Everglades cover more than 2,700 square miles (7,000 sq km). In places, saw grass grows almost 13 feet (4 m) tall. Elsewhere there are salt marshes and mangrove trees. No one lived in the swamps until the 1840s, when the Seminole Indians took refuge there. Some of the swamps have been drained for farming, and part forms a U.S. National Park, where visitors can see turtles, alligators, and many different kinds of birds. Like all wetlands, the Everglades need protecting to preserve their wildlife.

NORTH AMERICA FACTS
■ **Area:** 9,350,000 sq. mi. (24,211,000 sq km).
■ **Population:** 458,000,000.
■ **Number of countries:** 23 (including Central America and Caribbean).
■ **Longest river:** Mississippi, 2,350 mi.
■ **Largest lake:** Lake Superior, 31,700 sq. mi. (82,103 sq km).
■ **Highest mountain:** Mount McKinley (Alaska), 20,320 ft. (6,194 m).
■ **Largest country:** Canada.
■ **Country with most people:** United States.
■ **Largest city:** Mexico City; population of 16.5 million in 1996.

▶ **The St. Lawrence Seaway is one of the major transportation routes in North America, carrying manufactured goods and raw materials.**

A Florida alligator can sometimes be mistaken for a floating log—until it opens its mouth!

What is the Canadian Shield?

This is not a defensive weapon, but the biggest geological landform in Canada. It covers half the country. The Shield is an area of rock almost 600 million years old. It has rounded hills, many lakes and, in the south, thick conifer forests. Farther north it is too cold for trees. The Canadian Shield is an important mining region.

Where can ocean-going ships sail far inland?

Along the St. Lawrence Seaway, big ships can carry cargoes from the Atlantic Ocean as far inland as the Great Lakes—a distance of over 2,170 miles (3,500 km). The Seaway is made up of deepened and widened stretches of the St. Lawrence River and canals. It was opened in 1959.

What is the largest state in the United States?

The largest state is Alaska, which has an area of 586,500 square miles (1,519,000 sq km). That's four times the size of Germany.

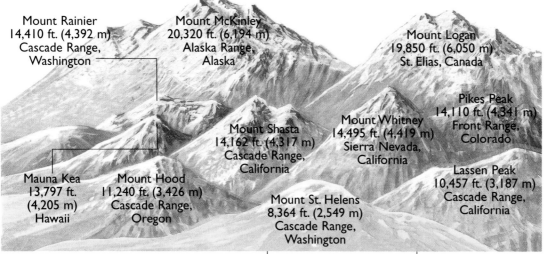

Mount Rainier
14,410 ft. (4,392 m)
Cascade Range,
Washington

Mount McKinley
20,320 ft. (6,194 m)
Alaska Range,
Alaska

Mount Logan
19,850 ft. (6,050 m)
St. Elias, Canada

Pikes Peak
14,110 ft. (4,341 m)
Front Range,
Colorado

Mount Shasta
14,162 ft. (4,317 m)
Cascade Range,
California

Mount Whitney
14,495 ft. (4,419 m)
Sierra Nevada,
California

Lassen Peak
10,457 ft. (3,187 m)
Cascade Range,
California

Mauna Kea
13,797 ft.
(4,205 m)
Hawaii

Mount Hood
11,240 ft. (3,426 m)
Cascade Range,
Oregon

Mount St. Helens
8,364 ft. (2,549 m)
Cascade Range,
Washington

The Hawaiian islands are part of the United States, even though they are in the Pacific Ocean. High volcanic mountains stick up out of the sea to form the islands.

Where is the highest mountain in North America?

Mount McKinley, in the Alaska Range, is in the northwest of the continent. It has two peaks, the higher rising to 20,320 feet (6,194 m). The mountain was named for William McKinley, the 25th President of the United States. Its original name is Denali, "the high one."

Where are the Rocky Mountains?

The Rocky Mountains form the largest mountain system in North America. They extend over 3,000 miles (4,800 km) from Canada into the United States. Most of the mountains were formed millions of years ago by movements of the Earth's crust.

Which river is known as the Big Muddy?

The Missouri is the second longest river in the United States. It carries vast amounts of mud, hence its nickname "Big Muddy." The Native American name Missouri is said to mean "town of the large canoes."

▲ The highest mountains in North America. Also included is Mauna Kea, in Hawaii.

▼ A Mississippi paddlewheel steamboat has a flat bottom, so it doesn't get stuck on sand banks. Steamboats used to carry passengers and cargo up and down the river. Today they carry tourists.

What is unusual about Mount Rushmore?

Mount Rushmore is a granite cliff in the Black Hills of South Dakota. Into the rock are carved four huge faces of U.S. presidents: George Washington, Thomas Jefferson, Theodore Roosevelt, and Abraham Lincoln. The head of George Washington is as high as a five-story building. A complete figure on this scale would be about 460 feet (140 m) high.

Where is the Panama Canal?

The Panama Canal cuts across the Isthmus of Panama (an isthmus is a narrow neck of land). The canal is 50 miles (80 km) long and was opened in 1914. Digging began in 1881, but

work stopped in 1889 because so many workers died of tropical diseases. In the early 1900s the United States took on the task, having leased the surrounding land from the new republic of Panama. Ships using the canal are saved a long journey around South America to sail from the Atlantic to the Pacific Ocean. After 2000 Panama will run the canal.

What are the Antilles?

There are two main groups of Caribbean islands—the Greater Antilles and, farther east, the Lesser Antilles. The islands of the Lesser Antilles are smaller; they include the Windward and Leeward Islands which curve southward.

Which is the largest island in the West Indies?

Cuba, the most westerly of the Greater Antilles islands, is the largest West Indian island. Next comes Hispaniola, which is divided into two countries: Haiti and the Dominican Republic (which occupies the eastern part of the island).

▼ **Native Americans made these leather moccasins and a pipe decorated with colorful, patterned weavings.**

Where do the Chippewa live?

The Chippewa are a group of Native Americans living in North Dakota and Minnesota. They originally lived around Lake Superior, in both the United States and Canada. The name of Manitoba (a province in Canada) is thought to have come from the Chippewa word *manitou*, meaning "great spirit."

What are moccasins?

Moccasins are traditional shoes made by Native Americans in North America. The Eastern Woodland tribes made moccasins from a single piece of leather, and often decorated them. Today, craftworkers continue these traditional skills for tourists.

Which Native Americans are famous weavers?

The Navajo people of the Southwest weave colorful wool blankets. They are the second largest tribe in the United States, second in numbers only to the Cherokee. They are successful in farming and business, earning money from coal mining, lumber, and manufacturing as well as from weaving and other craftwork.

▶ **Cuba is a long, thin island with the Atlantic Ocean on its northern shore. The United States still has a military base at Guantánamo Bay.**

Where is the Capitol?

The Capitol Building is in Washington, D.C. Both the Senate and the House of Representatives meet here. Work began on the building in 1792, but the dome was not completed until 1865.

Which U.S. cities have the tallest buildings?

New York City and Chicago are rivals in the skyscraper contest. New York has the World Trade Center and the Empire State Building, while Chicago (which claims to be the home of the skyscraper) has the taller Sears Tower, the second highest building in the world.

Where are yellow cabs a familiar sight?

Visitors to New York City can travel around the city in one of its famous yellow cabs. Or they can ride on one of the city's three subway systems. New York City also has two of the best-known railroad stations in the nation: Grand Central Terminal and Pennsylvania Station. Thousands of commuters travel to the city each day.

The President of the United States lives in the White House in Washington, D.C. It earned its name after the building was burned by British troops in 1814 and the smoke-stained walls were painted white.

▼ An Inuit. The name Eskimo (also used for the Inuit) is a Native American word meaning "eaters of raw meat."

◄ New York's brightly lit Times Square is one of the city's many famous sights. Many Broadway theaters are located in this area.

In which part of North America is French more common than English?

In the Canadian province of Quebec. Most of the people of Quebec are French Canadians. Montreal, the largest city in Quebec, has more French-speakers than any other city in the world after Paris in France.

Why do people come to watch the Calgary Stampede?

This is one of the most exciting rodeo shows in the world. It takes place in July every year in Calgary, a city in Alberta, Canada. Large crowds pack the arena to watch the famous chuck wagon race, which is one of the highlights of the rodeo.

Where do the Inuit live?

The Inuit are people who live in the Canadian Arctic. Here, most of the ground is covered by snow in winter. The Inuit traditionally lived by hunting and fishing, but the modern world has brought changes, including the mining of oil and gas. Many Inuit now have regular jobs or make craft goods to sell to tourists. They want more control over their ancient lands.

Where do people store corn in pyramids?

In Mexico. Cone-shaped silos looking somewhat like pyramids can store a year's corn harvest. The Mayan people grew corn as their main food crop in Mexico as early as 3,000 years ago, and it is still an important source of food, forming the basis of many Mexican dishes.

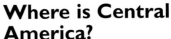

Where is Chichén Itzá?

Chichén Itzá is an ancient city in Mexico, built by the Mayan people over 1,000 years ago. The city's ruins include a tall limestone pyramid with a temple on top, and a huge plaza or open space where there was a steam bath and a ball game court. The ruins are now an important archaeological site and tourist attraction.

Where do people celebrate the Day of the Dead?

The Day of the Dead is a Mexican holiday which takes place every year on November 2nd, All Souls' Day. People remember dead friends and relatives, taking flowers and candles to their graves and having picnics there.

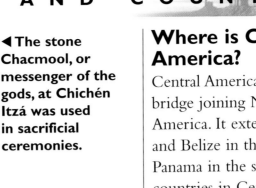

◀ The stone Chacmool, or messenger of the gods, at Chichén Itzá was used in sacrificial ceremonies.

FACTS ABOUT NORTH AMERICA

■ Mexico's most popular sport is soccer. Mexicans also enjoy bullfights.

■ A favorite dish in Newfoundland, Canada, is flipper pie (made from fish).

■ The first people to settle North America came from Asia more than 15,000 years ago.

■ The first Europeans known to have visited North America were Vikings, about the year A.D. 1000.

■ The United States is the fourth biggest country by area—after Russia, Canada, and China.

■ The national bird of the U.S. is the bald eagle, shown on the Great Seal of the United States.

▼ Mexicans make painted papier-mâché skeletons to celebrate the Day of the Dead. The skeletons wear hats, too!

Where is Central America?

Central America is the narrow land bridge joining North and South America. It extends from Guatemala and Belize in the north as far as Panama in the south. There are seven countries in Central America, the largest being Nicaragua.

Who built pyramids in Central America?

The native peoples of Central America developed remarkable civilizations. The Mayan people built great stepped pyramids. On top of each pyramid was a small temple. They also built cities such as Tikal, in what is now Guatemala. The great age of Mayan civilization lasted from A.D. 250 to 900.

How did the Caribbean Sea get its name?

The Caribbean Sea is to the east of Central America. Its name comes from the Caribs, a people who lived on some of the islands of the West Indies and in South America. When Christopher Columbus sailed to the Americas, in 1492, the Spanish sailors called the sea *Mar Caribe*— Caribbean Sea.

Where is cigar-rolling an important industry?

Cuba is famous for its cigars. Workers roll Havana cigars by hand. These cigars are named after the capital city of Cuba. Cuba has had a communist government since 1959, when Fidel Castro overthrew the dictator Fulgencio Batista.

SOUTH AMERICA

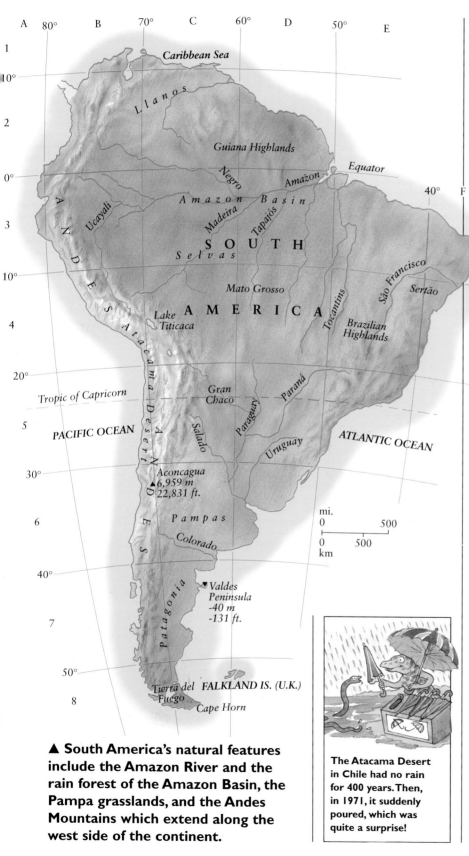

A 80°   B   70°   C   60°   D   50°   E

1

10°   Caribbean Sea

2   Llanos

Guiana Highlands

Negro   Amazon   Equator   40°   F

0°   A m a z o n   B a s i n

Ucayali

3   Madeira Tapajós

S O U T H

Selvas

10°   Mato Grosso   São Francisco   Sertão

4   Lake   A M E R I C A   Tocantins   Brazilian
           Titicaca   Highlands

20°   Gran   Paraná
Tropic of Capricorn   Chaco

5   PACIFIC OCEAN   Salado   Paraguay   ATLANTIC OCEAN
                                      Uruguay

30°   Aconcagua   mi.
           ▲6,959 m   0   500
           22,831 ft.
                                        0   500
6   P a m p a s   km

           Colorado

40°   ▼ Valdes
                       Peninsula
7   -40 m
                       -131 ft.

50°   Tierra del FALKLAND IS. (U.K.)
8   Fuego
                                        Cape Horn

▲ **South America's natural features
include the Amazon River and the
rain forest of the Amazon Basin, the
Pampa grasslands, and the Andes
Mountains which extend along the
west side of the continent.**

**The Atacama Desert
in Chile had no rain
for 400 years. Then,
in 1971, it suddenly
poured, which was
quite a surprise!**

Is South America south of North America?

The South American continent is actually southeast of North America, not directly south. New York, on the east coast of North America, is farther west than Valparaiso, Chile, on the west coast of South America.

How big is South America?

South America covers an area of nearly 7 million square miles (18 million sq km), so it is roughly twice as big as Canada. South America has the world's biggest rain forest, in the Amazon River Basin and the high Andes Mountains.

Where is Cape Horn?

Cape Horn is at the southernmost tip of South America. Most of South America lies within the tropics, yet Cape Horn is less than 620 miles (1,000 km) from Antarctica.

Who were the first people to live in South America?

When Europeans arrived in South America in the late 1400s, they discovered that people had been living there for thousands of years, including the great Aztec, Inca, and Mayan civilizations. Today, most South Americans are of mixed ancestry. They share many traditions, but local cultures reflect their African, American Indian, and European background.

Which are South America's most important rivers?

There are four mighty river systems in South America. They are the Magdalena, Orinoco, Amazon, and Paraná-Paraguay.

Why is Quito not so tropical?

Quito is the capital of Equador. It is only 15½ miles (25 km) south of the Equator so it should be hot. However, it is almost 10,000 feet (3,000 m) above sea level, which means it has a mild climate—higher means cooler.

Where is Patagonia?

Patagonia is a bleak desert region at the very southern tip of Argentina. When Spanish explorers reached it in the 1500s they met local Indians who stuffed their boots with grass for extra warmth. The name Patagonia comes from a Spanish word meaning "big feet."

▶ La Paz in Bolivia holds the record as the world's highest national capital.

SOUTH AMERICA FACTS

■ Area: 6,800,000 sq. mi. (17,817,000 sq km).

■ Population: 323,000,000.

■ Number of countries: 12.

■ Longest river: Amazon, 4,005 miles (6,448 km).

■ Largest lake: Maracaibo, 5,217 sq. mi. (13,512 sq km).

■ Highest mountain: Mount Aconcagua (Argentina), 22,831 ft. (6,959 m) above sea level.

■ Largest country: Brazil.

■ Country with most people: Brazil.

■ Largest city: São Paulo (Brazil).

▶ Glaciers flow down from the Andes Mountains. This is a glacier in Patagonia, seen from a viewing platform.

Which is the highest capital city in the world?

La Paz, the capital of Bolivia, is 11,800 feet (3,600 m) above sea level. High in the Andes, it is the world's highest capital. Lhasa in Tibet is higher by about 165 feet (50 m), but Tibet is no longer an independent country.

Which is the biggest lake in South America?

South America has fewer large lakes than other continents. The biggest lake is Lake Maracaibo (5,217 square miles [13,512 sq km]) in Venezuela. This lake has valuable oil reserves beneath it and is also a busy waterway.

How big is the Amazon rain forest?

The Amazon rain forest is one of the wonders of the natural world. The Amazon River Basin, in which the rain forest grows, covers about 2¾ million square miles (7 million sq km). That's twice the size of India. Although much of the forest has been destroyed by logging and burning, it is still by far the biggest forest anywhere on Earth. Conservationists are trying to save as much as possible of the remaining rain forest from destruction.

What is the Selva?

The Selva is a region of tropical rain forest in the Amazon River Basin. It is one of four regions in the central plains of South America. The other three are the Llanos grasslands of the north, the Gran Chaco scrub-forest, and the southern Pampas grasslands.

Where do gauchos live?

Gauchos are South American cowboys. Huge herds of cattle roam the grassy plains of Brazil, Uruguay, and Argentina. The gauchos used to be horsemen who rounded up wild cattle. Now they are ranch workers.

▶ The Amazon rain forest is amazingly rich in plant and animal life. Each layer of the forest teems with life, from the dark forest floor to the sunlit treetops.

▼ Gauchos look after enormous herds of cattle on the grassy plains of South America. They ride tough, well-trained horses.

Liana

Monkey

Frog

Toucan

Macaws

Butterfly

Ants

MORE FACTS ABOUT SOUTH AMERICA

■ Much of South America is thinly populated but cities such as São Paulo are fast-growing, with many poor people.

■ Coastal Peru and northern Chile are among the driest places on Earth.

■ Cape Horn at the tip of South America is only 600 mi. (970 km) from Antarctica.

■ Spanish is spoken in most of South America, except in Brazil where Portuguese is spoken.

■ The Amazon holds 20 percent of the world's fresh water.

■ Lake Titicaca in Bolivia is the highest lake in the world used by boats. It is 12,533 ft. (3,821 m) above sea level.

Why is South America a youthful continent?

South America has more than 450 million people. The population now is three times greater than 50 years ago. Many people have large families and about a third of all South Americans are under 15 years old.

Which is the biggest city in South America?

São Paulo, in Brazil, with a population of more than 16 million, is the largest South American city, yet it is not Brazil's capital. Brasilia, a new city with 400,000 people, replaced Rio de Janeiro as the capital in 1960.

Is South America rich in minerals?

Yes, the continent has large reserves of metals such as copper, iron ore, lead, zinc, and gold. Venezuela is the chief South American oil producer. Bolivia has tin mines. Guyana, Suriname, and Brazil mine bauxite (which is aluminum ore).

What does Cotopaxi do?

From time to time it erupts, for Cotopaxi is one of the world's largest active volcanoes. It has erupted 25 times in the past 400 years, the last time in 1975. Cotopaxi is in Ecuador and is 19,342 feet (5,897 m) high.

Where is South America's lowest point?

On the east coast of Argentina. The Valdés Peninsula is about 130 feet below sea level.

Why do some South American places have Dutch names?

In Suriname, on the northeast coast, the official language is Dutch. Suriname was once a Dutch colony. Most people in South America speak Spanish or Portuguese, the languages of Europeans who settled and conquered most of South America from around 1500. In French Guiana and Guyana, the people speak French and English.

Which part of South America has the hottest weather?

The Gran Chaco region of Argentina. Here it can get as hot as 109°F (43°C). Most of South America has its hottest weather in January, which is a summer month south of the Equator.

Climate
- Subpolar
  Very cold winter
- Mountainous
  Altitude affects climate
- Temperate/Marine
  Mild and wet
- Subtropical
  Warm with mild winter
- Tropical
  Hot with high rainfall
- Steppe
  Warm and dry
- Savannah
  Hot with dry season
- Arid
  Hot and very dry

Where does the Orinoco River flow?

This South American river flows through Venezuela in the north of the continent and empties its waters into the Atlantic. It forms the border between Venezuela and Colombia.

The Amazon rain forest is bigger than similar tropical forests in Africa and Asia. It spreads on either side of the enormous Amazon River.

▲ A map of the climate regions of South America. Most of the continent is warm with good rainfall.

Where is Sugar Loaf Mountain?

The Brazilian city of Rio de Janeiro is famous for its white sandy beaches, its carnival, and two mountain landmarks, known as Sugar Loaf (1,325 feet [404 m] high) and Corcovado (2,309 feet [704 m]). Sugar Loaf is a curious egg shape; on top of Corcovado is a 98-foot (30 m) statue of Jesus Christ.

▲ The statue of Jesus Christ above Rio de Janeiro, with Sugar Loaf Mountain in the background.

Where is the finest natural harbor in South America?

Despite having a very long coastline, South America has few bays suitable for use as harbors. The finest natural harbor is at Rio de Janeiro in Brazil.

Where are the world's longest mountains?

The Andes stretch more than 4,340 miles (7,000 km) along the western side of South America. They form the world's longest mountain range (not counting undersea mountains). Aconcagua in Argentina (22,831 feet [6,959 m]) is the highest peak.

Where is Machu Picchu?

The Inca city of Machu Picchu, high in the mountains of Peru, was never discovered by the Spanish invaders who conquered the Inca empire in the 1500s and 1600s. Today, the ruins of Machu Picchu are one of the most impressive monuments to the civilization of the Inca people.

Where is the world's highest waterfall?

The Angel Falls plummet down a cliff on Mount Auyantepui in southeast Venezuela. These falls are the highest in the world, with a total drop of 3,211 feet (979 m). The first sighting of the falls by a white person was by an American pilot named Jimmy Angel in 1935.

Who listened greedily to tales of El Dorado?

El Dorado ("The Golden Man") was a legendary Indian king. He was said to be so rich that he covered himself in gold dust. Tales of El Dorado encouraged explorers from Spain to travel across Central and South America in the 1500s and 1600s, seeking gold. They found gold, but did not find El Dorado.

▲ The ruins of the Inca fortress-city of Machu Picchu were discovered in 1911 by an American archaeologist.

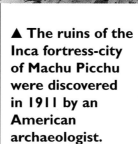

▲ Kamayura of the Amazon.

Where do the Kamayura people live?

The Kamayura are just one of the many native peoples who live in the rain forests of South America. The Kamayura live in Brazil, hunting and fishing in a way of life that remained unchanged for thousands of years until the 1900s.

Which Latin American countries grow coffee?

Coffee is a major crop in Colombia, Brazil, and Ecuador. The coffee beans are exported all over the world.

In which country do women wear distinctive hats?

In the Andes Mountains of Peru, women still wear traditional clothes, including shawls and highly distinctive hats that look somewhat like derbies. Men wear embroidered hats with ear flaps.

◄ Dusted with gold, El Dorado made a ritual voyage in a raft. This small gold raft is a reminder of a now-forgotten magical ceremony.

EUROPE

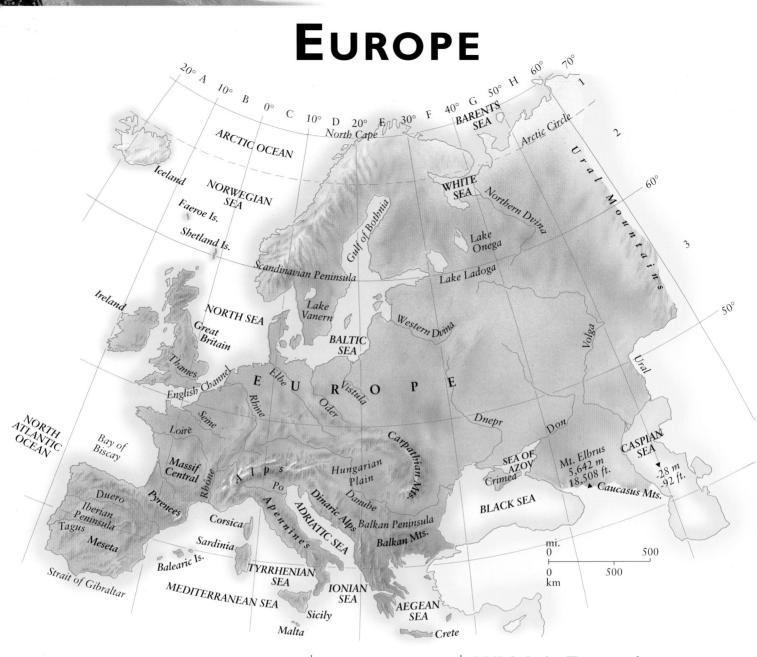

Where do Europe and Asia join?

Europe is part of the Asian landmass, because no sea divides it from Asia. In the east, several natural land barriers form a boundary between Europe and Asia. These barriers include the Ural Mountains, the Ural River, and the Caspian Sea. Since Europe and Asia are joined, the two together are sometimes referred to as Eurasia. Europe is smaller than all the other continents except Australia.

▲ The map of Europe shows how the continent has water on three sides. Its natural features include mountain ranges such as the Pyrenees, Alps, Carpathians, and Urals. Europe's rivers include the Danube, Rhine, and Volga.

Which is Europe's longest river?

The longest river in Europe is the Volga. It flows for over 2,190 miles (3,530 km) across Russia and empties into the Caspian Sea.

Why is western Europe ice-free in winter?

Although much of the coast of Norway lies in Arctic waters, it is not ice-bound in winter. Norway, like the rest of northwest Europe, has milder winters than places in North America that are equally far north. This is because the Gulf Stream's warm waters flow across the Atlantic. The warm ocean current warms the winds blowing from the sea across western Europe, keeping winters in coastal areas (such as Britain) mild, with ice-free oceans.

Where is Scandinavia?

Scandinavia is a region of northern Europe. Three countries are in Scandinavia, though not all of them are on the Scandinavian peninsula: Denmark (the most southerly), Norway, and Sweden. Sometimes Iceland (an island in the Atlantic Ocean), and Finland are also included.

Where is Lapland?

Lapland is the part of Scandinavia and Finland north of the Arctic Circle. It is not a country, but takes its name from the Lapps (or Sami), a people who traditionally roam the area with their herds of reindeer.

► The Black Forest in Germany is a reminder that in the past much of western Europe was covered by dense forest.

EUROPE FACTS

■ Area: 4,067,400 sq. mi. (10,534,600 sq km).

■ Population: 713,000,000.

■ Number of countries: 47.

■ Longest river: Volga, 2,193 mi. (3,531 km).

■ Largest lake: excluding Caspian Sea (Europe–Asia border) Lake Ladoga in Russia, 6,835 sq. mi.

■ Highest mountain: Mount Elbrus, 18,508 ft. above sea level.

■ Largest country: Russia (partially in Asia).

■ Country with most people: Russia.

■ Largest city: Moscow (Russia), 8,957,000 people.

◄ The Lapps still herd reindeer. These hardy people use the animals to draw sleds across the snow-covered ground.

Where is the Black Forest?

The Black Forest, or *Schwarzwald* in German, is a region of mountains and coniferous forest in southwest Germany. The Danube River rises there and the Rhine River flows along its western edge. The Black Forest, with its dark-leaved trees, is a remnant of the much larger forests that once covered most of northern Europe.

Why has the Mediterranean Sea been so important?

The Mediterranean Sea has been a trading area for thousands of years. Civilization spread across the sea from Egypt and Mesopotamia. Greece and Rome became powerful, and later Italian city-states such as Venice grew rich from Mediterranean trade. Today the Mediterranean is still important for trade, especially with the oil fields in the Middle East, and is also a popular tourist area. Around its sunny shores are busy ports, picturesque villages, and modern vacation resorts.

Map of Italy

SWITZERLAND
AUSTRIA
Lake Maggiore
Lake Como
Lake Garda
Bolzano
Trento
Udine
Dolomites
SLOVENIA
Monte Bianco 4,807 m 15,771 ft.
Como
Bergamo
Milan
Verona
Padua
Venice
Gulf of Venice
Trieste
Turin
Po
Ferrara
CROATIA
Parma
Reggio
Modena
Ravenna
Genoa
Bologna
Imola
Rimini
FRANCE
La Spezia
San Remo
Arno
Florence
SAN MARINO
Ancona
LIGURIAN SEA
Pisa
Leghorn
Siena
Arezzo
Perugia
Assisi
ADRIATIC SEA
Corsica (France)
Elba
Lake Trasimeno
Terni
Pescara
Civitavecchia
Tiv
Térmoli
VATICAN CITY
ROME
ITALY
Foggia
Barletta
Sassari
Olbia
Ponza
Naple
POMPEII
Bari
Brindisi
Ischia
Capri
Amalfi
Taranto
Lecce
Oristano
Sardinia
TYRRHENIAN SEA
Gulf of Taranto
Cape Santa Maria di Leuca
Cagliari
Cosenza
Strait of Bonifacio
Ustica
Stromboli
Lipari Is.
Catanzaro
MEDITERRANEAN SEA
IONIAN SEA
Trapani
Palermo
Messina
Reggio di Calabria
Marsala
Caltanissetta
Catania
Sicily
Pantelleria
Syracuse
Ragusa
Cape Passero

mi. 0 — 100
km 0 — 100

◄ **Italy is shaped somewhat like a boot. The north is cooler than the south, and more industrialized. The islands of Sicily and Sardinia are part of Italy.**

Is all of Italy warm?

Parts of Italy have a Mediterranean climate with mild winters and hot, dry summers. The south, especially Sicily, can be very hot. However, areas of northern Italy around the Po Valley and in the Alps have cold winters.

How high are the Scottish Highlands?

In the Highlands of Scotland are the highest mountains in Britain. They are ancient and have been worn and weathered over many millions of years, giving them a smooth, rounded appearance. The highest mountain, Ben Nevis, is only 4,406 feet (1,343 m) high.

▼ **Cannes is a quiet town when its famous film festival is not going on.**

Where is the Côte d'Azur?

In the south of France the summers are dry and hot, and there are usually many sunny winter days. The French call part of their Mediterranean coast the "sky-blue coast," or Côte d'Azur, for this reason.

Which European country has reclaimed nearly half its land from the sea?

The Netherlands. The name Netherlands means "low countries," and this part of Europe is very flat and low-lying. Sea walls called dykes hold back the sea. Pumps drain the flat land, and a network of canals carry the water away. Large areas of marsh have been reclaimed from the sea and turned into good farmland.

Which countries share the Iberian Peninsula?

Spain and Portugal. This square-shaped peninsula is in the southwest corner of Europe.

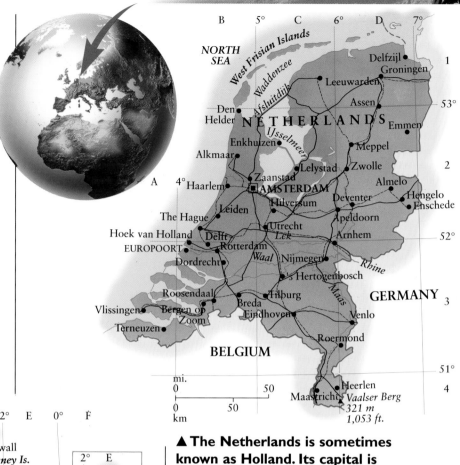

▲ The Netherlands is sometimes known as Holland. Its capital is Amsterdam.

Where is the Camargue?

The Camargue is the delta, or mouth, of the Rhône River in southeastern France. Formed by sedimentation, it is flat, lonely marshland, with numerous shallow lagoons. Rich in bird life, it was once known for its herds of horses and fighting bulls. Today farmers grow vines and rice there.

How many countries make up the British Isles?

Two: the United Kingdom and the Republic of Ireland. The United Kingdom consists of Great Britain (England, Wales, and Scotland) and Northern Ireland.

◄ This map shows the main natural features and cities of the United Kingdom. The capital is London.

Where does the Po River flow?

The Po flows in Italy, across the broad Lombardy plain south of the Alps. It is Italy's longest river.

Where are the Carpathian Mountains?

These mountains are in central Europe. They form part of the boundary between Slovakia and Poland, and extend into Romania. They are lower than the Alps, with a high point of 8,710 feet (2,655 m), and have fewer lakes, glaciers, and waterfalls. The Carpathians in Romania are said to be the home of the legendary Count Dracula!

Where is the land of a thousand lakes?

Finland, in northwest Europe, has about 60,000 lakes and thousands of offshore islands. Europe's biggest freshwater lake is not in Finland, however. It is Ladoga, in Russia.

Where is St. Petersburg?

This Russian city was made the capital of Russia by Emperor Peter the Great in 1712. In 1914 its name was changed to Petrograd and in 1924 it was renamed Leningrad, after the Soviet communist leader Lenin. It returned to its old name in 1991 after the fall of communism.

How long is Britain's longest river?

The rivers in Britain are not very long. The Severn, about 220 miles (350 km), is the longest. The Thames is slightly shorter, at 215 miles (346 km).

It takes eight days to cross Russia by train! As children go to school in Moscow (west), children in Vladivostok (east) are going home. Russia is so large it straddles both Europe and Asia.

EUROPE FACTS

- Vatican City in Rome, Italy, is the smallest state in the world.

- About one-eighth of the world's people live in Europe.

- After Russia, Ukraine is Europe's largest country. Next comes France.

- Europe takes its name from Europa, a princess in Ancient Greek mythology.

Where are the Balkans?

The Balkans are a group of countries on the Balkan Peninsula in southeast Europe, including Albania, Greece, Macedonia, and Bulgaria. To the east of the Balkans is the Black Sea and to the south is the Mediterranean. There are several mountain ranges in the area.

Where is the Corinth Canal?

This canal connects the Gulf of Corinth in southern Greece with the Aegean Sea. It was opened in 1893 and is the deepest canal ever cut. Its walls are 1,505 feet (459 m) high.

▶ Finland is a country in Scandinavia. Lapland is in the northern part of Finland.

◄ The Leaning Tower of Pisa is one of the world's curiosities. The problem facing engineers is how to keep it in one piece but still leaning!

What makes the Leaning Tower of Pisa lean?

The Leaning Tower is one of Italy's most remarkable landmarks. It is a marble bell tower built in Pisa between 1173 and the 1360s. Unfortunately, the builders chose ground that was too soft to carry such a weight, and the tower soon began to lean. It is already 16½ feet (5 m) out of vertical, despite efforts to hold it up, and engineers are considering new ways to stop it from falling.

What is Florence famous for?

Florence is a city in Italy with beautiful old buildings, paintings, and sculptures. It is a treasure-house of art and architecture. Tourists from all over the world come here to admire the art galleries, museums, and churches—including the Cathedral, known as the Duomo. Florence has a famous old bridge, the Ponte Vecchio, built across the Arno River in 1345.

Where is Venice?

Venice is an elegant city of islands and canals in Italy. It was once a rich city-state, whose rulers were known as *doges*. Venice is a unique city, where people travel by boat rather than by car, and is famous for its palaces and churches. Its annual carnival was at its grandest in the 1700s, and at carnival time people still dress up in costumes based on designs from that period. The city is endangered by seasonal floods which threaten its buildings and works of art.

▲ Michelangelo's statue of David is one of the many art treasures to be seen in Florence.

Why are houses in Amsterdam tall and narrow?

Amsterdam is a city in the Netherlands, also known as Holland. In the 1600s land for building was so scarce, and therefore prices so high, that merchants in the city built narrow but extremely tall houses—still a feature along the many canals of the attractive old city.

Where would you see stave churches?

In Norway. Stave churches are wooden churches, so-called because of the four wooden staves, or corner posts, around which they were built. Between 1000 and 1300, wooden stave churches were built all over Norway—not long after the Vikings who lived there were converted to Christianity.

◄ This stave church in Norway is almost 1,000 years old. It was built by Vikings.

AUSTRALASIA AND THE PACIFIC

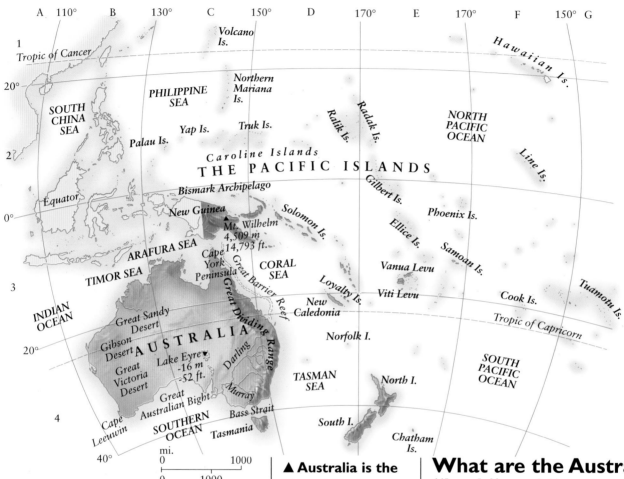

▲ Australia is the biggest landmass in the island region of the southern Pacific. There are thousands of other islands.

Where is Australasia?

Australia, New Zealand, and neighboring islands in the Pacific Ocean make up Australasia. Papua New Guinea is also included. Australia is sometimes treated as a continent on its own because it is so big. The islands excluding Australia are called Oceania. The whole area covers vast parts of the Pacific Ocean, from the warm seas north of the Equator to the icy waters around Antarctica.

What are the Australian "bush" and "outback?"

Most Australians today live in towns and cities. They call the countryside the bush and the vast, near-empty interior of their country the outback. The outback has a few mining and farm settlements, but no large cities. Most outback farms are cattle or sheep ranches, called "stations." Some are huge, covering more than 965 square miles (2,500 sq km)—bigger than a city the size of New York or London. Ranchers use trucks and helicopters and keep in touch with the outside world by radio.

Where is Tasmania?

Tasmania is an island about 125 miles (200 km) off the coast of southern Australia. The Bass Strait separates the island from the mainland. Tasmania was part of the mainland until about 12,000 years ago. It became an island when the sea rose, filling what is now the Bass Strait.

Which lake in Australia disappears?

A map of Australia shows Lake Eyre, an apparently large lake in South Australia. Yet most years the lake is dry. It fills with water only after unusually heavy rains. Most of the time it is a bed of salt. The salt forms a crust over 13 feet (4 m) thick.

The prickly-pear cactus, introduced to Australia, escaped from gardens and spread over thousands of miles. The caterpillars of the Cactoblastis moth finally destroyed it.

▶ The bed of Lake Eyre is a thick coating of salt. The salt forms lumps and patterns on the surface of the lake, which is usually dry.

Which is Australia's longest river?

The Murray (1,610 miles [2,589 km]) is Australia's longest permanently flowing river. The Darling is 1,700 miles (2,740 km), but much of it is dry in the winter. Early explorers had hoped to find greater rivers flowing from the vast heart of the country.

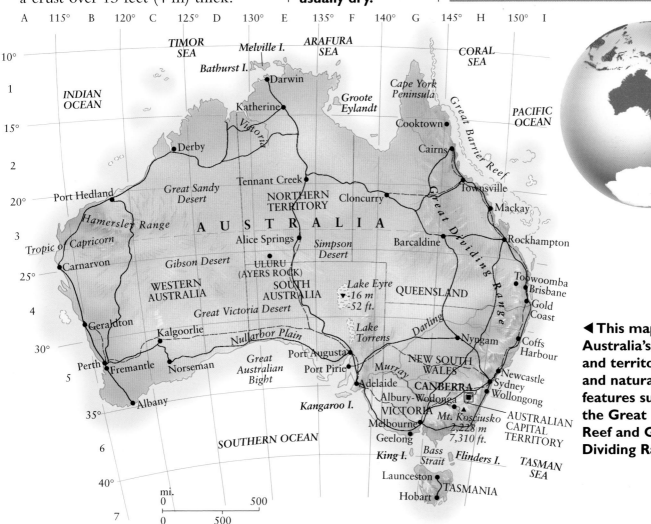

◀ This map shows Australia's states and territories, and natural features such as the Great Barrier Reef and Great Dividing Range.

After whom is Sydney, Australia, named?

In 1778 a party of British sailors and convicts landed in a bay in south Australia. They named it after Viscount Sydney, a British government minister. Sydney is now the largest city in Australia, and the harbor is famous for its bridge and opera house (an arts center).

Are there winter sports in Australia?

Mount Kosciusko in southeast Australia is the highest mountain of the country. It is a peak in the Snowy Mountains range in the Australian Alps and is 7,310 feet (2,228 m) high. In winter it is snow-covered and good for skiing.

Where are the Sutherland Falls?

The Sutherland Falls is one of New Zealand's many impressive waterfalls. Water plunges 190 feet (580 m) down a mountain near Milford Sound on South Island. The falls are the fifth highest in the world.

▲ The kiwi is an unusual bird of New Zealand. Kiwis live in burrows, coming out at night to look for grubs and worms to eat.

Even though Australia was not known in the Western world, it did exist in old myths. Terra Australis even appeared on early maps as a large round mass long before any European had seen it.

◄ Although much of Australia is too warm for snow, Mount Feathertop, one of the peaks running south from the Great Dividing Range, is high enough for snow.

► A waterfall in Milford Sound, a sea inlet on the west coast of South Island, New Zealand.

Where are people called "Kiwis?"

New Zealanders are often referred to as "Kiwis." The kiwi, a flightless bird, has become one of New Zealand's national emblems. New Zealand's wildlife includes a number of plants and animals found nowhere else in the world. It has some of the oldest plant forms known.

Which country has more sheep than people?

One of New Zealand's most important industries is sheep farming. There are about 71 million sheep in New Zealand—that's over 20 times the number of people. Australia has even more sheep, about 135 million, compared to over 17 million people. The wool industry in Australia was started in the late 1700s when settlers from Britain introduced merinos (a breed of sheep with fine wool).

◄ A geyser near Rotorua in New Zealand gushes steam and spray. Volcanic energy produces these hot waterspouts.

Where in New Zealand do rocks produce steam?

The North Island of New Zealand is a region of volcanic rocks. Heat from deep beneath the Earth warms underground water, which forces its way to the surface as geysers, jets of steam, and bubbling hot springs.

Why are some Pacific islands high, and others very low?

The high islands of the Pacific (such as Fiji) were made by volcanic activity on the ocean floor, which pushed up mountains. The low islands, such as Tuvalu, are coral reefs and atolls. Most are small, and some are so low that flood waves easily sweep over them.

AUSTRALASIA FACTS

- Area: 3,285,700 sq. mi. (8,510,000 sq km).
- Population: 29,000,000.
- Number of countries: 11.
- Longest river: Murray (Australia), 1,610 mi. (2,589 km).
- Largest lake: Lake Eyre (Australia), 3,700 sq. mi. (9,583 sq km).
- Highest mountain: Mount Wilhelm (Papua New Guinea), 14,793 ft. (4,509 m) above sea level.
- Largest country: Australia.
- Country with most people: Australia (over 17 million).
- Largest city: Sydney.
- Many marsupials live in Australia. The best known of these pouched animals is the kangaroo.
- Bats were the only mammals to reach New Zealand before people introduced domestic animals.

◄ In the warm, clear waters around the Pacific islands, coral reefs thrive. Many fish and plants live on or around the coral where there is safety and plenty of food to eat.

Where is Oceania?

Oceania is the name given to the thousands of islands scattered across the Pacific Ocean. Not all Pacific islands are part of Oceania. Indonesia, the Philippines, and Japan are part of Asia. Australia is either treated as a separate continent or grouped with nearby islands of Oceania under the name Australasia.

Which is the largest Pacific island?

New Guinea is the largest island in the Pacific and the third largest island in the world, with an area of 300,000 square miles (777,000 sq km). New Guinea and New Zealand together make up more than 80 percent of all the land in the Pacific islands. Many other Pacific islands are tiny.

▼ Islands of Palau in Micronesia, seen from the air. There are thousands of islands scattered across the ocean.

How many islands are there in the Pacific?

No one knows exactly how many islands there are in the Pacific Ocean. There may be as many as 30,000. Some are tiny islets or coral atolls just high enough to break above water.

Where is Polynesia?

The islands of the Pacific form three main groups. These are Melanesia in the southwest Pacific; Micronesia in the northeast Pacific; and Polynesia in the central and south Pacific. Polynesia means "many islands" and this group is the largest. The distance across Polynesia from Midway Island in the north to New Zealand in the south is over 5,000 miles (8,000 km).

Where do people throw boomerangs?

The boomerang is a wooden throwing stick used mainly by the Aborigines, the native people of Australia. Some boomerangs are shaped in a special way so that they return to the thrower. Others are made to stun or kill an animal being hunted for food.

What is mysterious about Easter Island?

Easter Island is an island in the Pacific Ocean, 2,200 miles (3,540 km) west of Chile. It is famous for very large stone statues of people. These huge carvings were made with stone axes by people who once lived on Easter Island but then moved away. Exactly why the statues were set up remains something of a mystery. The statues were probably made after A.D. 400 by people who came either from South America or Polynesia by boat. In the 1700s, following a war on the island, many statues were broken.

▶ **One of the mysterious huge stone heads found on Easter Island. Some 600 statues like this were carved from volcanic rock.**

Polynesian sailors explored the vast South Pacific Ocean in wooden canoes. The ancestors of the Maoris reached New Zealand by canoe about 1,000 years ago.

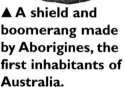

▲ **A shield and boomerang made by Aborigines, the first inhabitants of Australia.**

Where do people in neighboring villages speak different languages?

Papua New Guinea is a land of many languages. Most of the people live in small villages, deep in the forest or high up in the mountains. Some remote villages are so cut off from each other that their languages are quite different. People need a translator to speak to their neighbors on the other side of the mountain!

How do South Sea Islanders live?

The Pacific islands are small and isolated, and people depend mostly on farming, mining, and tourism. Islanders have traditionally lived from the sea, by fishing and trading.

Where are the Friendly Islands?

Tonga, an island kingdom in Polynesia, was given this name by the British explorer Captain James Cook. He landed there in 1773 and received a warm welcome.

What is pidgin English?

English is widely spoken throughout the Pacific, though French is used on some islands. In Melanesia, many people speak pidgin, a mixture of English and local words.

Which Pacific island group is part of the United States?

Hawaii. It was taken over by the United States in 1898 and became a state in 1959. Two of the volcanoes on Hawaii are still active.

GOVERNMENT

What is the United Nations?

The United Nations Organization, usually called the UN, is a group of many countries that joined together in 1945 to try to encourage peace in the world. The UN has 184 member countries, and its headquarters are in New York. The UN sometimes sends special forces to try to settle quarrels between countries. There are also several UN agencies, or international organizations, that deal with international social and economic problems around the world.

What is the Commonwealth?

When people talk about the Commonwealth, they usually mean the British Commonwealth of Nations. This is an association of nations that were once part of the British Empire. The British monarch is head of the Commonwealth, but the member countries are independent and govern themselves.

What is a republic?

A republic is a country in which the electorate (people allowed to vote) have the power to govern the country. The country is ruled by elected leaders. The head of a republic is usually called the president.

▶ The flag of the United States has stars for each state and 13 stripes (for the original 13 British colonies).

▲ Canadian troops arrive as UN peacekeepers in Sarajevo, one of the war-torn cities of the former Yugoslavia.

How many states are there in the United States?

The United States of America is a federal republic consisting of fifty states. Most of the states are next to each other in North America, but Alaska is separated from the rest by Canada, and Hawaii is an island group in the Pacific Ocean. The American flag has fifty stars on it. Each star represents one state.

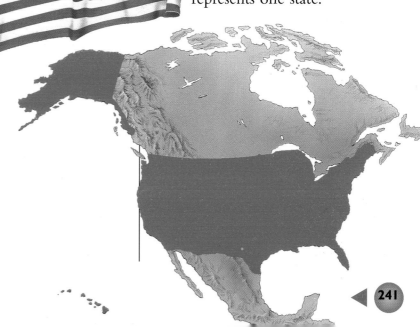

What does an ambassador do?

An ambassador is a person chosen by a country to represent it in another country. The ambassador lives in an embassy. He talks to the rulers and other important people in the country on behalf of the government of his own country.

What is a dictator?

A dictator is a ruler of a country who has total power over its people. In a country ruled by a dictator, called a dictatorship, there is usually only one official political party and no opposition is allowed. A dictatorship is often ruled by the army.

What is the European Union?

An organization of a number of European countries. The Union began in 1957 as the European Economic Community, also known as the Common Market. Its members seek to trade more freely with one another, and the Union also has a joint European Parliament and a Court. There are plans for a common currency, too.

▲ **Colonel Muammar Gadaffi has led Libya since 1969, as all-powerful president.**

▼ **Expensive stores like Tiffany's in New York City attract rich customers.**

Which countries belong to the European Union?

There are 15 members of the European Union. They are (with the dates they joined): Germany, France, Italy, Belgium, Netherlands, Luxembourg (all 1957); United Kingdom, Ireland, Denmark (all 1973); Greece (1981); Spain (1986); Portugal (1987); Austria, Sweden, and Finland (all 1995).

What is GNP?

GNP stands for Gross National Product. This means the amount of money a country earns in a year, minus its outgoings—such as imports and foreign debts. Divide by population to find the per capita (per head) figure.

◄ **Early designs for coins and travellers' checks for the new money system proposed for the European Union.**

Are people getting richer?

Some are, some aren't. Taking the world as a whole, average income per person has doubled since 1950. But while an American is three times richer today than in 1950, a person living in Ethiopia is no better off. The world's wealth is unfairly shared.

◄ **Gold ingots (bars) are kept in strongrooms under guard. Gold has been highly valued since ancient times and is still used as a measure of wealth.**

Every country has a national anthem. This is a special song which is sung to show respect for a country and its history.

Which country has the most gold?

The United States has about a quarter of the world's gold reserves. These are stored in gold bars at the U.S. Army base at Fort Knox in Kentucky under tight security.

Which is the richest country?

In terms of GNP per capita (per head), the answer is Switzerland, with a figure of $35,000. The poorest country is probably Mozambique where per capita GNP is less than $100.

Which is the world's biggest bank?

The World Bank, or the International Bank of Reconstruction and Development. It was founded in 1945. The Bank is an agency of the United Nations and lends money to countries for essential projects such as irrigation schemes to provide water for drinking and farm crops.

DID YOU KNOW?

■ Many countries besides the U.S. use the name "dollar" for their money.

■ But only Japan uses the *yen*. And only Poland uses the *zloty*.

■ The Chinese were the first to use paper money, in the A.D. 800s.

■ In Brazil, the richest 20 percent of the population earn 28 times more than the poorest 20 percent.

■ There are more than 170 self-governing countries.

■ There are about 60 colonies or other small territories ruled by larger nations.

■ The Ancient Greeks were the first people to experiment with democracy, or rule by the people.

What is communism?

A system of government and economics based on the ideas of Karl Marx (1818–1883), a German philosopher. The central idea of communism is that the government should run most businesses and own property for the good of all the people. In practice, communist states have usually been undem8cratic and badly managed, and by the 1990s only China, among the major nations, had a communist government.

What is federalism?

A union of self-governing states who agree to accept a single central government's rule in certain matters. Such a union is also known as a federation. Countries with federal systems of government include the United States, Canada, Australia, and Switzerland.

Which is the world's biggest democracy?

India, which has more than 500 million electors. The 1996 elections in India were the largest ever held in a democratic country.

Which country elects its king?

Malaysia. The king of Malaysia is the only elected monarch in the world. Other countries have kings, queens, sultans, sheikhs, or other rulers who hold the title through succession— which means each new ruler is a relative of the previous one. The eldest child of a hereditary ruler usually succeeds, but it can be the eldest son who takes over.

RELIGION AND CUSTOMS

Which Christian religion has the most followers?

The Roman Catholic Church has more followers than any other Christian religion in the world. Roman Catholics believe that the Pope is the successor of St. Peter, the apostle appointed by Jesus Christ to be head of the Church. The center of the Roman Catholic Church is Vatican City, in Rome, Italy. The Pope governs the Church from there.

▲ **Vatican City-State in Rome is the center of government of the Roman Catholic Church. It includes the great domed church of St. Peter.**

Siva

The Buddha

◀ **Siva is an important god in Hinduism. Hindus believe Siva is both creator and destroyer. Statues of the Buddha, founder of Buddhism, can be seen in many countries of Asia.**

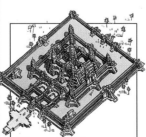

The world's biggest holy building is the 12th-century Hindu temple of Angkor Wat in Cambodia. It is 60 times as large as St. Peter's in Rome.

Which religions teach that people return to Earth after death?

Some religions teach that, after death, the soul or spirit of a human being enters another body, either human or animal. This belief is called reincarnation. Buddhists and Hindus, who live mainly in India, believe that their behavior in this life decides in what form they will be reborn. Some people believe that a person may be reborn many times until the soul is ready to enter heaven.

Which religion follows the teachings of the Koran?

The Koran is the holy book of Islam. In Islam, there is one god called Allah, and the Koran is believed to be the word of Allah which was revealed to Muhammad by the Angel Gabriel. Followers of Islam are known as Muslims. At least a million Muslims travel as pilgrims to the holy city of Mecca every year. This city in Saudi Arabia was the birthplace of Muhammad, and all Muslims try to go there once in their lives.

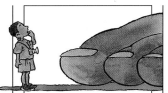

Who was Buddha?

Buddha, or "the enlightened one," is the title given to Siddhartha Gautama, an Indian holy man who lived in the 500s B.C. Buddha is believed to have sat under a tree called the Bo-Tree and come to understand the cause and cure of suffering. The followers of Buddha are called Buddhists. They live mainly in Southeast Asia, China, and Japan.

In 803, workers finished carving a statue of Buddha in cliffs near Leshan, in China. The statue is so big that two people can sit on one of its toenails!

Who is the head of the Church of England?

The king or queen of Great Britain is head of the Church of England (associated with the Episcopal Church). When Henry VIII quarreled with the Pope, he declared that the sovereign was head of the English Church, and this was later established by law.

What is a rabbi?

A rabbi is a specially ordained official who decides upon questions of law and ceremony in the Jewish religion, or Judaism. The rabbi performs marriages and other ceremonies and is similar to a priest.

BELIEF FACTS

■ The Jews were the first people to believe in one god, whom they called Yahweh.

■ Taoism, an ancient religion of China, has many gods. Some are famous people, others are ancestors.

■ Hindus celebrate a lively spring festival called Holi. People light bonfires and throw colored powder at one another.

■ Christmas trees are a reminder of old midwinter festivals, which have become part of Christmas.

▶ At Carnival time in Rio de Janeiro, Brazil, people in amazing costumes parade through the streets.

◀ Before his bar mitzvah, a Jewish boy receives instruction from a rabbi. The bar mitzvah marks acceptance into adulthood.

Why do people celebrate Halloween?

Halloween, on October 31st, is when children in the United States and some other countries dress up as witches, ghosts, skeletons, and scary monsters. Halloween comes from an old pagan festival that later became the Christian festival of All Saints' Day on November 1st. The religious mass (service) held on that day was called Allhallowmass and the evening before came to be known as Allhalloween. All Saints' Day is still a religious feast day in many Christian countries.

Why do people parade at Carnival time?

Carnival, or Mardi Gras, marks the start of Lent, a period of fasting for many Christians when they try to give up something (such as eating chocolate). In the past, Carnival was a celebration feast when people ate their last meal with meat before the solemn time of Lent began. Today people in bright costumes fill the streets for Carnival parades.

Why do we eat Easter eggs?

The eggs Christians exchange at Easter represent the renewal of life. Easter was originally a pagan spring festival, to celebrate the end of winter. Christians took it over and associated Easter with the resurrection, or rising from the dead, of Jesus Christ.

French children enjoy a special dinner on January 6th. Three kings from the East are said to have visited the baby Jesus on that day.

◄ **On Good Friday, Christians remember the death of Jesus on the cross. People in Ecuador parade a tableau of the event.**

▼ **Chinese people dance in dragon costumes to celebrate their New Year.**

What are saints' days?

In the Christian calendar some days are associated with saints. Examples are days named for patron saints of a country, such as St. Patrick's Day (Ireland) or St. David's Day (Wales).

What is Yom Kippur?

This is a Jewish festival. It is a day when people fast and express their regret for faults in their lives. It is also known as the Day of Atonement.

Which religion celebrates Diwali?

Hinduism. The festival of Diwali is a happy occasion when people enjoy parties, light candles, and give one another presents. It is a New Year festival dedicated to the god Vishnu and the goddess Lakshmi.

Who name their years after animals?

The Chinese New Year starts in January or February. In the Chinese calendar, which according to tradition begins in 2637 B.C., the years run in cycles of 60 and are named for 12 animals. 1997 was the year of the Ox, for example. The sequence continues as follows: Tiger, Hare (Rabbit), Dragon, Snake, Horse, Sheep (Goat), Monkey, Rooster, Dog, Pig, Rat.

What is Ramadan?

The month of fasting for Muslims. The end of Ramadan is marked by a holiday called the Eid, when people go to the mosque to perform special prayers of thanksgiving and entertain friends and family with enormous meals in their homes.

Why do Americans have parties on the Fourth of July?

Every July 4th, Americans celebrate Independence Day. All over the United States, people enjoy parades, picnics, pageants, and fireworks to mark the anniversary of the founding of the United States. Americans living abroad join in the celebrations.

What is Thanksgiving?

Thanksgiving Day is a national holiday in the United States and Canada. The first Thanksgiving was in 1621, when the Pilgrims in Plymouth Colony gave thanks to God for their first harvest. It is a time for family get-togethers and good food.

▲ **Muslims pray every day, often five times a day, turning to face toward Mecca as they do so.**

FURTHER FACTS

■ Since 1941, Thanksgiving Day has been on the fourth Thursday in November.

■ Easter is more important than Christmas to Christians in the Orthodox Churches.

■ December 26th is a holiday in some countries. It was traditionally a day for giving gifts, and so in Britain is called Boxing Day.

■ Scots celebrate Hogmanay on New Year's Eve, December 31st.

■ In many countries April Fool's Day, April 1st, is a day for playing jokes on one another.

■ St. Valentine's Day, February 14th, is a bonanza for the greeting card industry!

When is Bastille Day?

On July 14th, a special day for the people of France. French people celebrate Bastille Day in memory of an event during the French Revolution in 1789 when crowds stormed the Bastille prison in Paris. The prison was a hated symbol of the old, harsh government. Bastille Day is nowadays marked by a large military parade in Paris.

Is Buddha's birthday a festival?

In Japan, the Flower Festival is a colorful festival to mark the birth of Buddha. In Sri Lanka and Thailand, Buddhists celebrate Wesak or Vesakha-puja, a feast that marks not only Buddha's birth but also his enlightenment and death. Buddhism has largely disappeared from its country of origin, India.

▲ **Japanese people celebrate Buddha's birthday with flowers.**

PEOPLES AND COUNTRIES QUIZ

FIRSTS

When was the first voyage around the world?

In 1519 five ships left Spain. Three years later, one returned. It had sailed around the world. The leader of the historic expedition was Ferdinand Magellan (1480–1521), a Portuguese sailor. Like most of his seamen, he did not live to see its end. After crossing the Pacific, he was killed in a fight with local people in the Philippines.

Which European sailor first reached India?

In 1498 a Portuguese named Vasco da Gama arrived in India. Guided by an Arab sea captain, he was the first European seaman to land there.

Where was the Northwest Passage?

By the 1500s many people guessed that the world was round. By sailing west, across the Atlantic Ocean, a ship ought to be able to reach Asia. Even after the Americas were discovered, many tried to find the Northwest Passage. Finally, in 1906, a Norwegian ship commanded by Roald Amundsen (1872–1928) made the journey, from east to west, north of Canada.

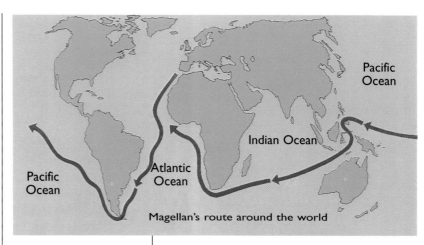

Pacific Ocean

Indian Ocean

Atlantic Ocean

Pacific Ocean

Magellan's route around the world

▲ A map of Magellan's historic voyage. His ships sailed around the tip of South America and across the Pacific Ocean. The survivors finally crossed the Indian Ocean on their way home.

We can't flap our arms fast enough to fly like birds. Our arm muscles are too weak. But people tried in vain to copy birds in the days before planes were invented!

Who made the first powered flight?

A balloon can fly only where the wind takes it. In 1852 a French aviator tried fitting an engine to a balloon. The aviator's name was Henri Giffard (1825–1882). His "airship" was a cigar-shaped balloon filled with hydrogen gas. It was powered by a small steam engine.

Who built the first successful airplane?

In the late 1800s many inventors tried to build a machine with wings and propellers that would fly under its own power. Pioneer fliers such as Otto Lilienthal (1848–1896) of Germany proved that a glider would carry a person into the air. Orville and Wilbur Wright built their own gliders, then added a homemade engine. In 1903 they made the first controlled flights in a heavier-than-air machine.

◀ The Wright brothers built their *Flyer* airplane themselves. It flew for just 12 seconds on its first flight.

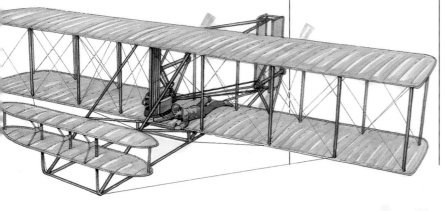

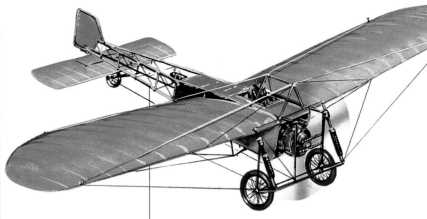

Who first flew from France to England?

In 1909 Louis Blériot (1872–1936), a French pilot, landed his airplane near Dover. He had made the first ever flight from France to England. Without a map or compass, Blériot got lost in a mist. His engine overheated, but a rain shower cooled it, and also cleared the mist. Spotting the Dover cliffs below, Blériot flew down to make a very bumpy landing after his 37-minute flight.

Who first used an aqualung?

Jacques Cousteau (1910–1997), a French naval officer, wanted to be able to swim freely under water. To do this, he and his team invented the aqualung. The diver carried air-tanks on his back, and swam with flippers on his feet. Cousteau proved that people could explore and even work under the sea.

Who were the first people to leave the Earth?

The first person to fly into space was the Russian Yuri Gagarin in 1961. In 1968 three U.S. astronauts flew around the Moon in *Apollo 8*. They were the first to escape from Earth's gravity.

▲ **Louis Blériot flew across the English Channel in a plane that he had designed and built. His flight made him famous in Britain and France.**

In 1958 the USS *Nautilus*, the first nuclear-powered submarine, sailed from the Bering Strait to Iceland, crossing directly under the North Pole. The journey took four days.

▶ **The first team of explorers to reach the South Pole was led by the Norwegian Roald Amundsen. Using huskies to pull their sleds, they reached the South Pole in Dec 1911.**

◀ **Russian cosmonaut Yuri Gagarin flew once around the Earth inside this *Vostok* spacecraft.**

Who first reached the North Pole?

The American explorers Frederick Cook and Robert Peary both claimed to have reached the North Pole—the first in 1908 and the second a year later. However, it is possible that their claims are not true and that they turned back before getting to the Pole. The first person definitely to reach the North Pole was the American explorer Richard Byrd, who, with his co-pilot Floyd Bennett, flew over the Pole in an airplane on May 9, 1926. The first explorer definitely to travel over the ice to the North Pole was the American explorer Ralph Plaisted. He arrived there on April 19, 1968.

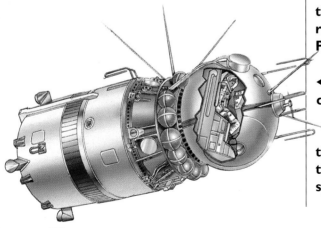

Who were the first people to cross Australia?

The center of Australia is desert, and it is dangerous to cross it overland. The first to make the journey, from south to north, were Robert Burke, William Wills, Charles Gray, and John King in 1860 and 1861. On the return journey, the explorers suffered hunger, thirst, exhaustion, and

sickness. They failed to make contact with other members of the exhibition and Gray, Burke, and Wills died. King lived with Aborigines and was rescued.

Who first swam the English Channel?

A British sea captain, Matthew Webb (1843–1883), first swam across the Channel from England to France, a distance of 21 miles (34 km) in a straight line. His swim, in 1875, took 21¾ hours.

▶ **New Zealander Edmund Hillary and Nepali Tenzing Norgay were the first to climb Everest, or *Chomo-Lungma* as the Tibetans call Everest.**

EXPLORING FIRSTS

■ Roald Amundsen of Norway led the first expedition to reach the South Pole in 1911.

■ In 1993 Erling Kagge of Norway walked alone to the South Pole.

■ From 1979 to 1982 explorers traveled to the South Pole, the North Pole and back to London —34,700 mi. (56,000 km).

■ The longest recorded swim was 1,825 mi. (2,938 km) down the Mississippi River in 1930.

■ The first European sailor to see the Indian Ocean was Bartholomeu Diaz of Portugal, who in 1487 sailed to the southern tip of Africa.

■ Around A.D. 800 the Maoris sailed in canoes across the Pacific from Polynesia to New Zealand.

◀ **The explorers crossing Australia used camels. These desert animals could survive in the hot, dry conditions of the Australian interior.**

Who first flew nonstop across the Atlantic Ocean?

Two British pilots, John Alcock (1892–1919) and Arthur Brown (1886–1948), made the first nonstop flight across the Atlantic Ocean in 1919. It lasted nearly 16½ hours, and Brown had to crawl out onto the wings of the airplane to remove ice that was forming there. The American pilot Charles Lindbergh (1902–1974) made the first solo crossing, in 1927.

Who first sailed around the world alone?

An American sailor, Captain Joshua Slocum (1844–c.1910), made the first solo voyage around the world in a small sailing boat called *Spray*. It took three years and two months, from 1895 to 1898.

Who first climbed Mount Everest?

Many people had tried and failed to climb the world's highest mountain before 1953. Two members of a British Commonwealth expedition reached the top on May 29, 1953.

EXPLORERS

Who discovered the Americas, but thought it was Asia?

The first European explorer known to have reached the Americas was Christopher Columbus, who was born in Italy but explored for the Spanish. He sailed from Spain to the Bahama Islands, off the coast of North America in 1492. Columbus was trying to find a new route to India or the Indies (then a name for the East), and thought he had arrived there. He therefore called the people he found there "Indians."

Who sailed across the Pacific on a raft?

In 1947, a team of scientists led by the Norwegian Thor Heyerdahl (born 1914) sailed across the Pacific Ocean on a raft called the *Kon-Tiki*. The raft was of an ancient design, and the trip showed that the people of the South Sea Islands could have gotten there by raft from South America.

Who are the Americas named after?

The Americas are named after the Italian explorer Amerigo Vespucci (1451–1512). Vespucci explored South America after Columbus reached the Americas. Vespucci believed that a new land had been discovered, and it was named "America" after him. The name was given to the two new continents— North and South America.

Christopher Columbus

▲ **Columbus set out with three small ships across the Atlantic. The journey to the New World took 30 days.**

In Columbus's time, many people believed the world was flat. They feared that he and his ships would sail too far west and fall over the edge!

▶ **Marco Polo followed the ancient trade routes across Asia to China. Travelers rode horses and camels over mountains and deserts.**

Where did Marco Polo travel?

Marco Polo (1254–1324) and his family were the greatest European travelers of the Middle Ages. Marco was born in Venice, Italy. His father and uncle were traders and had visited China, where they met the Emperor Kublai Khan. In 1271, they set off again with Marco. The travelers did not return until 1295. During all this time, they traveled throughout China and southern Asia. They were amazed by the sights they saw.

Who named a huge country after a village?

This was the French explorer Jacques Cartier (1491–1557) and the country is Canada. Although he was not the first European to reach Canada, Cartier was the first to explore much of it. From 1534 onward, he made three voyages to Canada. He tried to find out what the Native American name for the country was. However, the people he asked thought he was inquiring about their village. So they said "*kanada*," which meant "village."

▶ James Cook visited Pacific islands where local people came out to meet his ship in huge canoes.

▼ The Aztecs of Mexico thought Cortés was a pale-skinned god and welcomed him with gifts.

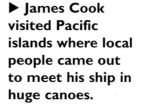

Who were the conquistadors?

The conquistadors were the Spanish invaders who conquered the Indian civilizations in Central and South America in the 1500s. *Conquistador* is the Spanish word for "conqueror." The conquistadors sought the gold treasures made by the Indians but destroyed their civilizations. The best known of the conquistadors are Hernando Cortés, who plundered Mexico, and Francisco Pizarro, who destroyed the Inca Empire of Peru. The invaders ruined the way of life of the peoples they conquered.

DID YOU KNOW?

■ Magellan had 277 men under his command when he set sail in 1519.

■ One ship and 19 men returned home in 1522 after the historic around-the-world voyage.

■ The first European to see the Pacific Ocean was the Spaniard Vasco Nuñez de Balboa.

■ In 1513 Balboa crossed Panama from the Atlantic coast and saw the Pacific.

■ Europeans had been to North America before Columbus. In A.D. 1000, the Viking Leif Ericsson sailed from Greenland to Newfoundland.

Who first explored the South Seas?

The South Seas are the southern part of the Pacific Ocean, and are dotted with many tropical islands. This part of the world was first thoroughly explored by Captain James Cook (1728–1779), a British explorer who made three voyages there between 1768 and 1779. He also explored Australia and New Zealand, and he realized that a great unknown continent (Antarctica) must exist to the south, though he never reached it. Cook was a great explorer. He made maps of the coastlines he sailed along, and on his ships were artists who drew the people, animals, and plants they saw. On his third voyage, Cook was murdered by islanders in Hawaii.

Who was Abel Tasman?

In 1642 sailors on board a Dutch ship sighted New Zealand. The ship's captain was Abel Janszoon Tasman (1603?–1659), the first European explorer to reach New Zealand and the island of Tasmania (named after him). Tasman was searching for an unknown "south land." He actually sailed around Australia without realizing it, and thought neither New Zealand nor Tasmania worth further voyages.

Who was Ibn Battuta?

Ibn Battuta was a great Arab traveler. During the 1300s, he visited many lands. He was shipwrecked, crossed the Sahara, and was entertained by kings and princes. He visited Egypt, Africa, Persia (Iran), India, Russia, Mongolia, and China. He went wherever there were fellow Muslims, including Spain (then partly under Moorish rule). Ibn Battuta was a scholar, curious always to see new sights, and his travels lasted 30 years.

Ibn Battuta was so famous that he was welcomed everywhere he went. He wrote a best-selling book about his journeys to many lands.

Who first explored Louisiana?

In the 1500s and 1600s, French explorers in North America opened up routes westward and south, into what is now the United States. Robert de la Salle (1643–1687) explored the Great Lakes by boat, and in 1682 he sailed down the Mississippi River to claim Louisiana for the French king, Louis XIV.

When did the Vikings reach North America?

North America was probably first sighted in about A.D. 986 by a Viking named Bjarni Herjolfsson, but the first visit was by Leif Ericsson in A.D. 1000. Leif reached the coast of Labrador and cruised south until he came to a land where wild grapes grew. He called it Vinland, after these vines. Vikings who tried to settle were driven out by Native Americans.

▶ A cathedral window shows David Livingstone, explorer and fighter against slavery in central Africa.

▼ The Vikings who landed in Vinland ("Vineland") hoped it would be a good place to settle and build new homes.

Where did Jedediah Smith explore?

In the early days of the American West, fur trader Jedediah Smith (1799–1831) made long trips into the wilderness.

Smith followed Native American trails from the Great Salt Lake west to the Rocky Mountains and on to California.

Who was David Livingstone?

In the 1800s Africa was still largely unexplored by Europeans. A Scottish missionary named David Livingstone (1813–1873) was a great African explorer. He also did much to end the evil slave trade. In 1866 Livingstone set off to search for the source of the Nile. Nothing was heard of him until 1871, when an expedition led by Henry Morton Stanley (1841–1904) found him near Lake Tanganyika. Though ill, Livingstone explored until the end of his life.

Who was Alexander von Humboldt?

Humboldt (1769–1859) was a German traveler and scientist, whose work was an example to other geographers. He trained as an engineer, but in 1799 he went off to South America. With him went his friend, the French botanist (plant expert) Aimé Bonpland (1773–1858). Humboldt and Bonpland hacked their way through the Amazon jungle and climbed the Andes Mountains.

Where did Lewis and Clark explore?

Two U.S. Army officers, Meriwether Lewis and William Clark, made a pioneer mapmaking journey across North America from 1804 to 1806. They led an expedition from St. Louis up the Missouri River and across the Rocky Mountains. They then explored the Columbia River westward to the Pacific Ocean, before returning to the East. Lewis and Clark mapped much new territory in the West, blazing trails for future settlers who went to California and other western territories.

▶ The bathyscaphe *Trieste* made its recordbreaking dive in 1960 with two people aboard. They rode in the cabin beneath the huge float.

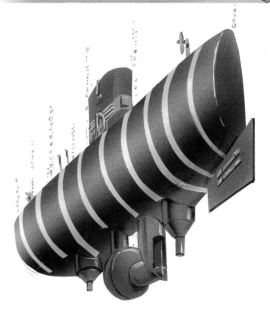

DID YOU KNOW?

■ Marco Polo was only 17 when he made the long, difficult journey from Europe to China.

■ Livingstone was the first European to see the Victoria Falls in Africa.

■ Livingstone and other explorers searched for the source of the Nile River.

■ In 1863 John Hanning Speke proved that the river's source was Lake Victoria.

■ The farthest any explorers have traveled is to the Moon. The first to land on the moon were U.S. astronauts Neil Armstrong and Edwin Aldrin in 1969.

■ The first Europeans to reach the Rocky Mountains were probably two French brothers, the Vérendryes, in the 1740s.

■ The name Sacagawea means "Bird Woman." Sacagawea was captured as a young girl and sold to a fur trader, later employed by Lewis and Clark.

Where did Jacques Piccard explore?

Jacques Piccard (born 1922), a Swiss scientist, dived into the deepest part of the Pacific Ocean. He used a special diving craft known as a bathyscaphe, and with a U.S. Navy officer, Don Walsh, made a record-breaking descent of 35,800 feet (10,900 m) into the Mariana Trench, the deepest valley on the ocean floor.

Who first crossed Antarctica?

In 1957 and 1958, an expedition crossed Antarctica using snow tractors instead of dog sleds as earlier explorers had. The expedition was led by a British scientist, Sir Vivien Fuchs (born 1908), and the journey took 99 days.

◀ Meriwether Lewis and William Clark were helped by a Shoshoni named Sacagawea. She acted as interpreter whenever they met other Native Americans.

RULERS AND LEADERS

Who was Julius Caesar?

Gaius Julius Caesar (100–44 B.C.) was a brilliant Roman general and writer who became the ruler of Rome. Caesar was a member of an aristocratic Roman family. He became joint ruler of Rome, and won greater fame by his success as a soldier. He conquered Gaul (France) and twice landed in Britain.

In 49 B.C. Caesar returned to Rome and made himself dictator. He campaigned in Egypt, where he fell in love with its queen, Cleopatra. Although he ruled Rome wisely, he had enemies who were jealous of his success. In 44 B.C. they assassinated him, claiming that he planned to make himself king of Rome.

▲ Boudicca led her people into battle against the Roman armies. After early successes, the Celtic Britons were defeated.

When Muhammad was fleeing from Mecca to Medina, he hid from his pursuers in a cave. While he was in there, a spider spun a web across the entrance. His pursuers saw the intact web and decided Muhammad could not be in the cave.

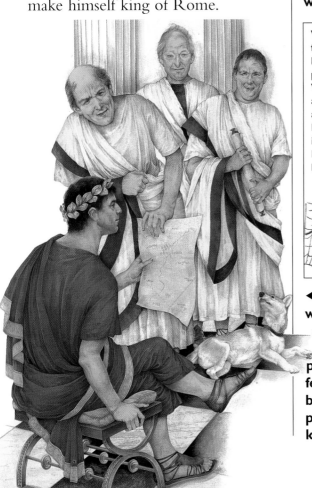

◀ Julius Caesar was Rome's most successful general. His political enemies feared he would become all-powerful, and killed him.

Who was Queen Boudicca?

Boudicca—sometimes called Boadicea—was ruler of the Iceni, a Celtic British tribe, in about A.D. 60. She led a rebellion against Roman rule in southern Britain. The rebels captured several towns including Londinium (London), but were then defeated by the strong Roman army. Boudicca poisoned herself rather than risk capture.

Who was Muhammad?

Muhammad was the founder of the Islamic religion. Its followers, the Muslims, call him the Prophet of God. The Prophet was born in Mecca, now in Saudi Arabia, in about A.D. 570.

In 595, Muhammad married a rich widow, Khadija. He led a peaceful life as a merchant in Mecca. When he was about 40 he had a vision of the Archangel Gabriel, calling him to preach the word of God. He began preaching in 613. In

620 Khadija died. By this time Muhammad had made many enemies and he was forced to flee. He took refuge at the oasis of Yathrib, now Medina, city of the prophet.

By 630 Muhammad had established his new religion. He died in 632. His teachings were recorded in the Koran, the sacred book of Islam, as revelations from God.

◄ Muslims believe the Archangel Gabriel was Allah's (God's) messenger. This painting shows Gabriel.

▼ A statue of Charlemagne. He led the most powerful empire in Europe.

Who was Charlemagne?

Charlemagne, born in 742, was king of the Franks (French) from 771 to 814. He made himself ruler of much of western Europe and attempted to revive the Roman Empire. On Christmas Day 800 Pope Leo III crowned Charlemagne Emperor of the West. Charlemagne was a great admirer of learning. He encouraged literature and the arts at the Frankish court, and founded a school at Aachen (now in Germany). He was a wise ruler. His empire, later called the Holy Roman Empire, lasted in various forms for about 1,000 years.

► This medieval picture shows William the Conqueror and the next three Norman kings: William II, Henry I, and Stephen.

Who was William the Conqueror?

William (c.1028–1087) was Duke of Normandy, in France. In 1066 he conquered England. William had a slight claim to the English throne. It is said that he was promised it by the Saxon king, Edward the Confessor, who had no heir, but when Edward died the English chose instead a Saxon earl, Harold, as king. So William invaded England and defeated the Saxons at the Battle of Hastings. Harold was killed in the battle.

Who was Saladin?

Saladin (1138–1193) was the greatest Saracen (Muslim) general at the time of the Third Crusade. He became sultan of Syria and Egypt, and in 1187 he captured the holy city of Jerusalem. When news of his victory reached western Europe the Third Crusade was proclaimed.

Who was Good Queen Bess?

Queen Elizabeth I of England is sometimes called Good Queen Bess. She was born in 1533, the daughter of King Henry VIII and Anne Boleyn, and became queen when her half-sister Mary I died in 1558. During Elizabeth's reign England became a great nation. She died in 1603.

Who was known as the Sun King?

Louis XIV of France was known as the Sun King. He became king in 1643 when he was only five years old. He was called the Sun King because his court was so splendid. He had a magnificent palace and gardens built at Versailles, near Paris. He remained king of France for 72 years and died in 1715.

▲ Queen Elizabeth reviews her troops at Tilbury, near London, before the sea battle against the Spanish Armada. Her fighting words inspired the English.

Who built the Taj Mahal?

One of the most beautiful buildings in the world, the Taj Mahal, was built at Agra in northern India by Emperor Shah Jehan. It took 20,000 workers about 18 years to complete (from 1630 to 1648) and was a tomb for his wife Mumtaz Mahal. She was Shah Jehan's favorite wife but died in childbirth. He was buried beside her beneath a great white dome which, on the inside, is 79 feet (24 m) high.

▼ King Louis XIV ruled France from his palace at Versailles. He approved plans for the lavish building and the costly entertainment put on there.

Which king of England had six wives?

Henry VIII. In 1509, he married Catherine of Aragon. He divorced her in 1533 and married Anne Boleyn. In 1536, he had Anne beheaded and immediately married Jane Seymour. She died the following year. His fourth wife was Anne of Cleves. He married her in 1540, and divorced her six months later. In the same year he married Catherine Howard, only to have her beheaded less than two years later. His sixth wife, Catherine Parr, managed to outlive him.

GREAT RULERS
■ Solomon (from about 1015 B.C. to about 977 B.C.), king of Israel. Famous for his wisdom.
■ Alfred the Great (849–899), king of the West Saxons in England. Fought the Vikings, made good laws, encouraged learning.
■ Genghis Khan (1162–1227), Mongol conqueror, founder of the largest land empire ever seen.
■ Akbar (1542–1605), Mogul emperor of India. Famous for his justice and religious tolerance.
■ Abraham Lincoln (1809–1865), President of the United States. Opposed slavery and led the Union to victory in the Civil War.

◄ **Henry VIII desperately wanted a son to rule England after him. If a wife failed to give him one, or displeased him in some way, he got rid of her.**

▼ **George Washington had fought on the same side as the British. Now he fought against them, to win independence for the United States. After the war, he was elected president.**

Who drafted the Declaration of Independence?

The first draft of the Declaration was made by Thomas Jefferson, a delegate to the Continental Congress of the 13 American Colonies in 1776. Jefferson was born in 1743 and became a lawyer. He began his political career in the Virginia Assembly. In 1783 he was elected to Congress; that same year he devised America's decimal currency. Jefferson then followed Benjamin Franklin as U.S. Ambassador to France; four years later he became Secretary of State. After that he was elected vice-president (from 1797 to 1801) and president (from 1801 to 1809). As president, he bought Louisiana from France. He died in 1826.

Who was the first President of the United States?

The first president was George Washington, who had led the armies of the American Revolution. He served from 1789 to 1797. Washington was born in Virginia in 1732. He worked as a land surveyor, fought in the French and Indian War, and then became a gentleman-farmer. When war started between Britain and its 13 American colonies, Washington was chosen as the American commander-in-chief. After the war was won, Washington helped draw up the U.S. constitution.

Who was known as "the grandmother of Europe?"

Queen Victoria was born in 1819 and became queen of Great Britain and Ireland in 1837. She reigned for nearly 64 years until her death in 1901. In 1840, Victoria married Prince Albert of Saxe-Coburg. Through her own marriage and those of her children, she was related to most of the royal families of Europe. For this reason, Victoria became known as "the grandmother of Europe."

Who crowned himself emperor of France?

Napoleon Bonaparte (1769–1821) was a Corsican soldier who crowned himself emperor of France in 1804. He was eventually defeated by British and Prussian forces at the Battle of Waterloo in 1815 and was exiled to the island of St. Helena in the South Atlantic.

Which king tried to make the waters obey him?

King Canute of Denmark and Norway became king of England in 1016. In order to demonstrate to his lords that his power was limited, he once took them to the seashore and commanded the tide to turn back.

Which ruler once worked as a shipbuilder?

Peter the Great (1672–1725) of Russia visited several European countries in his youth. He had a passion for ships and worked in shipyards in Holland and England.

Sitting Bull

▲ A painting of Napoleon by Jacques-Louis David, showing him as a heroic war leader. Napoleon came to power as a defender of the French Revolution against foreign enemies. He went on to bring other parts of Europe under French rule.

Who was Sitting Bull?

Sitting Bull was a fierce leader of the Sioux. He lived from about 1834 to 1890. So that they would not lose all their lands, Sitting Bull persuaded the Sioux to fight and kill the white settlers. This led to the famous Battle of the Little Bighorn in 1876, when the Sioux killed Colonel George Custer and his troops. This was the Native Americans' greatest victory. Sitting Bull survived the battle, but he was driven into Canada. He later returned to the United States and, still rebellious, was killed while resisting arrest.

Who was known as the Iron Chancellor?

Prince Otto von Bismarck, who created the nation of Germany, was known as the Iron Chancellor. He was born in 1815, when Germany was not one country but a league of separate states, and became chief minister of Prussia, the most powerful state. Then, after a series of wars, he united the states in 1871 into one Germany, of which he became Chancellor (prime minister). Because Bismarck said that problems should be settled by "blood and iron," he became known as the Iron Chancellor. He led Germany until 1890 and died in 1898.

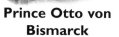

Prince Otto von Bismarck

◄ Franklin Roosevelt was famous for his radio broadcasts to the American people. He suggested the name United Nations for the allies during World War II.

Who was elected President of the United States four times?

Franklin D. Roosevelt, born in 1882, was elected President of the United States four times—in 1932, 1936, 1940, and 1944. He died in 1945, having served as president for twelve years, a record. Roosevelt was a remarkable man. He led the United States through the Depression of the 1930s and through World War II, yet he was crippled by polio and could not walk unaided. Now, no president may serve for more than eight consecutive years.

Who led Germany in World War II?

The German leader in World War II was Adolf Hitler (1889–1945). Hitler came to power in Germany in 1933 as the head of the National Socialist party. He and his followers were known as Nazis (short for National Socialists). They set up a dictatorship in Germany, killing their enemies, and invading other European countries. This caused World War II.

◄ Franklin Roosevelt was famous for his radio broadcasts to the American people. He suggested the name United Nations for the allies during World War II.

▲ Martin Luther King was a fearless campaigner for civil rights.

▼ Adolf Hitler dreamed of world domination. He led Germany into war, and ordered the killing of millions of innocent people.

Who led Britain in World War II?

The British leader in World War II was Winston Churchill, who lived from 1874 to 1965. Churchill became prime minister in 1940, soon after the outbreak of war. By then, Germany had invaded most of Europe, and Britain stood virtually alone against the enemy. The British forces fought strongly under Churchill's powerful leadership, and the country was not invaded. The U.S.S.R. and the United States entered the war in 1941, and four years later the war was over.

Which country was led by General de Gaulle?

Charles de Gaulle was the greatest French leader of this century. Born in 1890, he became a general early in World War II. When the Germans occupied France, de Gaulle refused to collaborate with them. He left, and commanded the Free French forces outside France. De Gaulle returned after the war, and was president of France from 1945 to 1946 and from 1958 to 1969.

Who was Martin Luther King?

Martin Luther King, Jr., led the civil rights movement in the United States, and won international acclaim for his campaign to win equal rights for African-Americans. King was a Baptist minister. He began his protests in 1955 when he led a boycott of buses in Montgomery, Alabama, because black people were made to sit in the rear seats. King believed in nonviolent protest.

THE ANCIENT WORLD

What is Stonehenge?

Stonehenge is an ancient monument in southern England. It was constructed at various times between 1750 B.C. and 1500 B.C. It was probably used as a temple, or to observe the movements of the Sun and Moon to make calendars.

Why were the pyramids of Egypt built?

The pyramids were built as tombs for the pharaohs (rulers) of Ancient Egypt, and they had chambers that contained the remains of the pharaohs. However, these chambers were later robbed of their treasures. The biggest pyramid, the Great Pyramid at Giza, was 480 feet high when built, around 2600 B.C.

▼ The Seven Wonders of the World were listed by writers in ancient times. They were visited by travelers who marveled at their size and magnificence. The pyramids were the oldest and by far the biggest of the Wonders.

What were the Seven Wonders of the World?

The Seven Wonders were structures of the ancient world. They were considered to be the seven most wonderful ever built. The Great Pyramid in Egypt is the only one still standing. The other six were the Hanging Gardens of Babylon; the Temple of Diana at Ephesus; the Tomb of Mausolus at Halicarnassus; the statue of Zeus at Olympia; the Pharos Lighthouse at Alexandria; and the Colossus of Rhodes, a statue beside the harbor entrance. There are no reliable pictures of the six vanished Wonders, only descriptions by historians and travelers.

Hanging Gardens of Babylon (Iraq)

The Great Pyramid at Giza (Egypt)

The Pharos Lighthouse at Alexandria (Egypt)

The Tomb of Mausolus at Halicarnassus (Turkey)

The Temple of Diana at Ephesus (Turkey)

The statue of Zeus at Olympia (Greece)

The Colossus of Rhodes (Greece)

Who founded the ancient city of Alexandria?

The city of Alexandria in Egypt was founded in 331 B.C. by the Greek emperor Alexander the Great (356–323 B.C.). By conquest, Alexander built up a great empire that extended from Greece as far as India and Egypt and was as big as the United States. The empire brought Greek civilization to the ancient world, and Alexandria became its center of learning.

Who was the first Roman emperor?

Augustus, who lived from 63 B.C. to A.D. 14, was the first emperor of Ancient Rome. Before Augustus, Rome was a republic governed by elected consuls. After the death of Julius Caesar, Augustus—then called Octavian—held power with Mark Antony (c.83–30 B.C.). Octavian defeated Mark Antony, and in 27 B.C. declared that Rome would be an empire with himself as the first emperor. He took the name Augustus, and Rome reached its greatest glory under his rule. The month of August is named after him.

◄ Alexander the Great led his armies as far east as India. In a short but brilliant life, he was never defeated in battle.

▼ Cleopatra lived in great splendor in Egypt. She was a descendant of one of Alexander the Great's generals.

DID YOU KNOW?

■ The Greek philosopher Aristotle was Alexander the Great's tutor.

■ Cleopatra married two of her brothers, sharing the throne with them.

■ She had a son by Julius Caesar, and twins by Mark Antony.

■ Hadrian's Wall had gates where soldiers kept a check on all people traveling in and out of Roman Britain.

Who was Cleopatra?

Cleopatra was an extremely beautiful queen of Egypt. She was born in 69 B.C. The Roman leader Julius Caesar, fascinated by her, made her queen. After Caesar's death, Cleopatra captivated Mark Antony, his successor. Antony left his wife, Octavia, for Cleopatra, provoking a battle for control of Rome with Octavian, who was Octavia's brother. Octavian met Antony and Cleopatra in battle in 31 B.C. and won. Defeated, Antony killed himself and Cleopatra soon also took her own life, possibly with an asp (a poisonous snake).

Why did the Romans build a wall across England?

Hadrian's Wall is a famous landmark in the north of England. It is a huge wall, 73 miles (118 km) long, which runs across the whole country from coast to coast. It was built by the Roman emperor Hadrian between A.D. 123 and 138 to keep Scottish raiders from invading England, then a province of the Roman Empire.

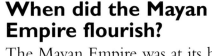
Who took elephants across the Alps?

Hannibal (247–182 B.C.) led the forces of Carthage against Rome and used elephants in war to scare his enemies. He took the Romans by surprise by marching over the Alps in 218 B.C., taking the elephants with him. Once in Italy, Hannibal harassed the Romans for years, but he did not defeat them.

▼ Hannibal's army and war elephants crossed the Alps.

Who were the Incas?

The ancestors of the Incas lived among the mountains of Peru possibly as long as 4,000 years ago. The Incas began building up their country in about A.D. 1200.

From 1438 to 1493, two kings, Pachacuti and his son Topa Inca, expanded the Inca Empire. It eventually covered large parts of present-day Ecuador, Bolivia, Chile, and Argentina.

Who were the Celts?

The Celts were a group of peoples living in central Europe in the 500s B.C. Many migrated west. They were warriors and farmers. Their language survives in Welsh, Gaelic, and Breton.

The Mayan people of Central America chewed gum. The rubbery gum was called chicle, and they collected it from the sapodilla tree. Chicle is still used to make chewing gum.

When did the Mayan Empire flourish?

The Mayan Empire was at its height in southern Mexico and Central America from about A.D. 250 to 900. The Maya built huge stone cities, had elaborate religious ceremonies, and developed a system of picture writing. The great Mayan cities were abandoned in the late 800s. Nobody knows why.

Who was China's first emperor?

For 260 years the states of eastern China fought each other for control of the whole country. The struggle was eventually won by Ch'in, one of the westernmost states. Its leader was Prince Cheng, known as the "Tiger of Ch'in." When Ch'in won, Cheng proclaimed himself Shih Huang-ti, which means "the first emperor." Shih Huang-ti also ordered the building of the Great Wall of China to keep out invaders from the north.

▶ The Inca ruler Pachacuti led his army into battle to expand his empire.

When was the Han dynasty founded?

The Han dynasty overthrew the Ch'in dynasty in 202 B.C. It ruled China for more than 400 years. During the Han dynasty the Chinese Empire expanded. Han scholars studied higher mathematics and astronomy. Paper was invented during this period, and Han traders visited Persia and Rome.

▼ **The Ancient Chinese built large cities. People from the countryside brought vegetables and farm animals into town to sell in the market. Travelers from the West were amazed by Chinese cities, and the orderly life that went on in them.**

Who was Attila?

Attila (*c.*406–453) was the leader of the Huns, a warlike group of tribes from central Asia that terrorized Europe in the A.D. 400s. He forced the rulers of the eastern Roman Empire to pay him a large annual fee to leave them alone. He then led a large army of Huns into Gaul (France). The Romans defeated Attila at Châlons-sur-Marne in 451. He died two years later.

Who was Confucius?

Confucius was a Chinese philosopher who lived 2,500 years ago (551–479 B.C.). The real name of Confucius was K'ung ch'iu. He became known as K'ung-fu-tzu, which means great master Kung; Confucius is a Westernized form of that title.

DID YOU KNOW?

■ The Vikings were feared as warriors. They hired themselves out as paid soldiers.

■ Much of what we know about Ancient China comes from tombs. Clay models of houses, soldiers, and horses have been found in Chinese tombs.

■ The Holy Roman Empire lasted until the early 1800s. But it was never very powerful after the Middle Ages.

■ Confucius believed in order, family, and good government. His ideas had a great influence on Chinese life.

■ The Huns were one of a number of "barbarian" peoples who attacked the Roman Empire. The Romans regarded these people as uncivilized.

▼ **Vikings fighting at sea. Their wooden longships were fast and easy to steer.**

Who were the Vikings?

The Vikings were pirates from Scandinavia. They were bold and skillful navigators, who sailed the European seas in their long ships. Each ship had a large, square sail, but could also be driven by oars.

From A.D. 793 onward, Vikings from Norway raided England. They began to settle there in the late 800s. Other Vikings attacked France and settled there. They were known as Northmen, or Normans, and gave their name to Normandy. Other Vikings reached Spain, Sicily, Italy, and Russia, leaving their mark.

What was the Holy Roman Empire?

The Holy Roman Empire was a group of small German and neighboring states that were powerful in the Middle Ages. It was intended to be a second Roman Empire built of Christian states. The empire was founded by Charlemagne, or Charles the Great, who was crowned the first Holy Roman emperor by the Pope in Rome on Christmas Day, A.D. 800.

FAMOUS EVENTS

What does the Bayeux Tapestry show?

The Bayeux Tapestry is a very long piece of embroidery. It shows in pictures the invasion of England by Duke William of Normandy (William the Conqueror) in 1066. Bayeux is a small town in northern France, and the tapestry is in a museum there. It is something like a comic strip. It starts with King Harold of England's visit to Duke William, probably in 1064. It ends with the Battle of Hastings in 1066 when Harold was killed by an arrow that pierced his eye, and his troops were defeated.

Sheep were brought to Australia by the early settlers. Today there are about 135 million sheep, nearly nine times the number of people in Australia!

▲ Norman soldiers on horseback charge into battle. This scene is part of the long Bayeux Tapestry, which tells the story of William's invasion of England in 1066.

Why is the year 1901 important in the history of Australia?

On January 1, 1901, the Commonwealth of Australia came into being. Before this, Australia consisted of a number of separate colonies. With the Commonwealth Act of 1900, the colonies became a federation. The formation of the Commonwealth marked the beginning of Australia as a full nation.

▶ Disguised as Native Americans, colonists threw British tea into the water. This was one of the acts that lead to the American Revolution.

What was the Boston Tea Party?

In 1773, when the U.S. was still a group of British colonies, a Tea Act was passed in Britain that allowed the East India Company to send tea directly from London to America without using American merchants. In Boston, a group of patriotic Americans boarded the tea ships and threw the tea into the harbor in protest. This defiant act became known as the "Boston Tea Party."

What was the charge of the Light Brigade?

Between 1854 and 1856 the Crimean War was fought between Russia on one side and Turkey, England, France, and Sardinia on the other. In October 1854 the Russians tried to seize the British base at Balaklava. Because of a misunderstanding of orders, the Light Brigade, an army division, charged the main Russian position. The soldiers were heavily outnumbered by the Russians and many were killed, but the brave survivors got through and captured the enemy position.

What caused the Civil War?

Political differences between the northern states (the Union) and the southern states (the Confederacy). The turning point came in 1860 when Abraham Lincoln became president. The South, which depended on slaves for labor, feared that Lincoln would abolish slavery. In 1861, 11 southern states separated from the Union because they thought that states, not Congress, should decide their own laws. After four years of fighting, the South surrendered, preserving the Union.

When was the Battle of Gettysburg?

The Battle of Gettysburg was a turning point in the Civil War. It lasted from July 1 to July 3, 1863. Gettysburg is a little town in Pennsylvania. The Confederates, led by Robert E. Lee (1807–1870), were defeated by the Union army under George Meade (1815–1872).

▲ **During World War I, recruiting posters urged men to join the army. Many died in trench warfare in France and Belgium.**

▼ **The Battle of Agincourt (1415) was an English victory over a larger French army during the long Hundred Years' War.**

Which war became known as the Great War?

World War I (1914–1918) became known as the Great War. This was because, at the time, there had never been a war in which so many different countries took part. More people were killed than ever before in a war, and more buildings were destroyed. But when World War II took place (1939–1945), it was even bigger and more destructive.

What was the Hundred Years' War?

France and England were at war from 1337 to 1453. This is more than a hundred years, but the period is known as the Hundred Years' War. It was eventually won by France.

Which event does the Eiffel Tower commemorate?

The Eiffel Tower, designed by A. Gustave Eiffel (1832–1923), was built for the Paris Exhibition of 1889. This exhibition commemorated the French Revolution, which began a century before. The Revolution started on July 14, 1789, when a mob of angry Parisians attacked the Bastille, a prison. They pulled the building down stone by stone. The anniversary of the destruction of the Bastille is a national holiday in France.

Which "unsinkable" ship sank on its first voyage?

This ship was the *Titanic*, a British passenger liner. At the time, the *Titanic* was the world's largest ship, and experts believed that it was unsinkable. But on the night of April 14, 1912, during its first voyage, it hit an iceberg in the middle of the Atlantic Ocean and sank. Out of more than 2,200 people on board, some 1,500 were drowned.

▲ In Paris, on July 14, 1789, crowds attacked the Bastille prison and freed all of the prisoners.

▶ Sitting beside his wife, Jacqueline, President Kennedy was driven through the streets of Dallas to meet the cheering crowds. Moments later he was shot by an assassin. People still argue about who killed him.

In the 1780s French people were angered by a new tax on salt, which they used to keep meat fresh. The tax made salt too expensive.

Who was shot at Ford's Theater in 1865?

Abraham Lincoln, sixteenth President of the United States, was fatally shot on April 14, 1865, at Ford's Theater, Washington, D.C. His assassin was John Wilkes Booth (1838–1865), a southern actor, who hated Lincoln for having defeated the Confederacy. He got into the presidential box, shot the president, then leaped onto the stage and fled. He was later captured.

When was President Kennedy assassinated?

President John F. Kennedy was assassinated by a gunman in Dallas, Texas, on November 22, 1963. The President was being driven in an open car.

Who won the Battle of the Little Bighorn?

The battle was fought on June 25, 1876, between the Sioux and a U.S. cavalry column led by Colonel George A. Custer. Trouble had begun in 1874 when the United States government sent miners and soldiers into the Black Hills of South Dakota, a region sacred to the Sioux. The Sioux refused to sell the land, so the government decided to drive them out. Custer split his force of 650 troops into three columns. His own column fell into a Sioux ambush led by Chief Sitting Bull. Custer and his men were all killed.

▼ On D-Day, June 6, 1944, Allied troops landed in France. The massive air, sea, and land invasion was the biggest in history.

When did World War II start?

World War II began with the German invasion of Poland on September 1, 1939. On September 3, Britain and France declared war on Germany. Australia, New Zealand, India, Canada, and South Africa supported Britain. By 1940 Germany had overrun much of Europe. Japan and Italy joined in on Germany's side. Italy invaded Yugoslavia, Greece, and much of North Africa. Germany then attacked Russia in 1941, the year the United States entered the war. In 1944 Allied forces invaded western Europe while Russia attacked from the east. Germany was defeated by May 1945. Japan surrendered in August 1945.

▼ Genghis Khan's Mongol warriors rode into battle on horseback. Each man was a skilled rider and fighter.

What happened at Pearl Harbor?

On the morning of December 7, 1941, Japanese bombers attacked the United States naval base at Pearl Harbor, Hawaii. They destroyed six warships, damaged 12 others, and destroyed 174 aircraft. The Japanese attacked while their officials were negotiating in Washington, D.C. about causes of dispute between Japan and the United States. The Pearl Harbor attack took the United States into the war against Japan and its allies, Germany and Italy.

Which empire was ruled by Genghis Khan?

Genghis Khan (1162–1227) was the leader of the Mongols, a warlike group of people from central Asia. He was one of the greatest conquerors in history, leading a vast army against China in 1211 and into Russia in 1223, and threatening to overrun eastern Europe. Genghis Khan created a Mongol empire. His grandson Kublai Khan (1215–1294) ruled China.

What was the Spanish Armada?

The Armada was an invasion fleet of galleons packed with soldiers sent from Spain to attack England in 1588. Spain was then Europe's mightiest power. The English fleet fought off the Armada in a series of battles in the English Channel, but did not seriously damage it. However, the Spanish could not join forces with an invasion army waiting in the Netherlands, and their ships were driven north around Britain by strong winds. Many were wrecked in storms off the coasts of Scotland and Ireland.

When did the Pilgrim Fathers land in America?

In 1620 a group of Puritans left England on a ship called the *Mayflower*. They were bound for new lives in America. They sailed from Plymouth in England and landed in Massachusetts. The Pilgrim Fathers, as they became known, founded

▲ **The great galleons of the Spanish Armada were out-sailed by the smaller English ships at the Battle of Gravelines in the English Channel.**

the second English colony in North America (after Jamestown, Virginia, 1607)—the first was founded by people seeking religious freedom. Those who survived the hard winter gave thanks for their first harvest with a feast—the first Thanksgiving.

When did France become a republic?

In 1792, after revolution had overthrown the monarchy. The French Revolution began in 1789, as a movement to make government in France more democratic. But the revolution rapidly became more extreme and violent. People accused of being enemies of the republic were executed. In 1799, a soldier named Napoleon Bonaparte seized power, and he soon made himself emperor.

◄ **The Pilgrim Fathers were helped by Native Americans as they built homes and planted crops in their new land.**

When was the Russian Revolution?

In 1917, revolutionaries forced the czar (emperor) of Russia to give up his supreme power. A group of communist extremists, known as Bolsheviks, seized power from the liberal democratic politicians. Their leader was Vladimir Lenin (Vladimir Ilyich Ulyanov; 1870–1924). By 1921, Lenin had made Russia a communist state, the largest of the new Union of Soviet Socialist Republics.

Who led India to independence?

Mohandas Karamchand Gandhi (1869–1948) was the most influential leader of the movement that won India's independence from British rule in 1947. Gandhi was a lawyer, who preached a policy of nonviolence as he campaigned for India's freedom. After independence, Gandhi tried to stop the fighting that broke out between India's Hindus and Muslims. He was assassinated in 1948 by a Hindu who disliked Gandhi's tolerance of all religions.

GREAT EVENTS

■ Greece fought a war for freedom against Turkey from 1821 to 1829.

■ Spain's colonies in South America won their independence between 1809 and 1825.

■ 1848 became known as Europe's Year of Revolutions.

■ In 1860 Giuseppe Garibaldi led a victorious army from Sicily through southern Italy to join up with King Victor Emmanuel's army from the north. When Rome was captured, Italy became a united country.

■ Fidel Castro led the Cuban Revolution of 1959 which overthrew the dictator Fulgencio Batista.

■ In 1900 only two African countries—Ethiopia and Liberia—were truly independent. By the 1990s all the major territories of Africa were self-governing.

◀ **Gandhi first practiced nonviolent protest in South Africa. He took his beliefs to India and inspired other protestors around the world.**

▶ **South Africa's Nelson Mandela with Queen Elizabeth II of Great Britain. Mandela won praise for his courage and statesmanship.**

When was Germany reunited?

Germany was divided by the victorious Allies after its defeat in World War II (1939–1945). East Germany came under communist rule and Russian domination, while West Germany was rebuilt by the Western democracies as a prosperous, free country. In 1961 the building of the Berlin Wall symbolized the division of the two Germanies. In 1989, the collapse of communism in Eastern Europe began. The government in East Germany fell, the Berlin Wall was torn down, and in 1990 Germany became one country again with a democratic government.

Who was South Africa's first black president?

From the 1950s, all South Africans were classified by race. Whites ruled, while blacks had few freedoms. Nelson Mandela, a leader of the African National Congress, was jailed from 1962 until 1990 for opposing the government. As the old system broke down, he was freed, and in 1994 he was elected South Africa's first black president.

HOW PEOPLE LIVED

When did cities first have real drains?

The people of Ancient India, China, and Rome built good water-supply systems. They even had public baths. Mohenjo-Daro in Pakistan, was built about 4,000 years ago. This city had drains to bring in fresh water and sewers to carry away waste.

When did people first make bricks?

Bricks were first made over 6,000 years ago. They were shaped from wet mud and dried in the Sun's heat. Brickmaking began on the river-banks of the Near East and Mesopotamia. The bricks we use today are probably not very different in size from those used in ancient times. The builders of Babylon decorated their bricks, making wall-pictures or mosaics. Later, bricks were hardened by baking them in a kiln, or oven, in the same way as pottery is baked. Brick houses were stronger than houses made of wood.

Brickmakers in ancient times trampled river mud with their bare feet until it was sticky. They added bits of straw to make the mixture stronger and used wooden molds to shape the bricks.

▶ **The ruins of Mohenjo-Daro, one of the first cities planned with a street grid and real drains.**

▼ **The people of Babylon (a land in what is now Iraq) built pyramid-shaped ziggurats, or temples of brick.**

When was the first alphabet invented?

The Phoenicians, living in the eastern Mediterranean some 3,500 years ago, were the first to invent an alphabet of sound-signs. Their alphabet was borrowed and improved by first the Greeks and then the Romans. Our word "alphabet" comes from the Greek words for the first two letters in their alphabet, *alpha* and *beta*.

When did people first shop in supermarkets?

The first department store, offering many goods beneath one roof, was opened in Paris in 1860. The first supermarkets, selling all kinds of goods in a single store, opened in the United States in the 1930s. In some places supermarkets have driven smaller shops out of business.

When did people use oil lamps?

Fat burns, and the sight of this probably caused a cave dweller to make the first oil lamp. Animal fat and oil gave people light for thousands of years, until an improved kind of oil lamp was invented. In 1784 a Swiss named Aimé Argand (1755–1803) invented an improved oil lamp. It had a glass chimney to shield the wick, and it gave a much brighter light. In the 1800s many homes were lit only by kerosene lamps. Gas and electric lighting were introduced later.

When were carpets first made?

The first floor coverings were mats woven from rushes. Weaving skills were later used to make rugs and carpets from wool. The finest carpets were richly patterned and very valuable. Carpets made more than 2,000 years ago have been found in tombs in Asia.

When did people first eat with knives and forks?

Cheap factorymade knives and forks appeared on dining tables in the 1800s. Before then, only rich people used them. Most people ate with their fingers at mealtimes. In the Middle Ages travelers took their own knives with them. Guests would expect to be offered a knife only if they were dining with a very rich person. Table forks were even less common until the 1700s.

When did frozen foods first appear?

Before people had freezers, they stored winter ice in stone ice houses. The Romans made ice cream. A method of making artificial ice was invented in 1834 by Jacob Perkins. By the 1850s refrigerated ships were carrying frozen meat across the oceans. People in Europe could eat meat that came from Australia or the Americas. Frozen foods, such as frozen fish and vegetables, were introduced in the 1920s, when people began to buy freezers for their homes.

DID YOU KNOW?

- In the city of Ur (modern Iraq), an arch of bricks was built about 4000 B.C.

- The Romans burned petroleum in their oil lamps.

- In the 1680s oil lamps were used to light London streets.

- All carpets were woven by hand until the 1700s, when factory machines were invented to make them more quickly.

- Until the 1400s, few people ate off plates. They used a thick slice of bread, called a trencher.

- The Romans used two-pronged forks at the table.

- Travelers in the 1700s carried a fork, spoon, and mug in a special case.

▼ Diners at a feast in the Middle Ages ate with their fingers. Servants brought the various dishes to each person. Bones were thrown to the dogs.

When did people first read newspapers?

In the Middle Ages, news of a foreign war, or the king's death, often took days to reach distant parts of the country. Town criers shouted out the news to townsfolk. In the 1500s, after the invention of printing machinery, people began reading pamphlets and newsletters. The first newspaper to be printed regularly was called the *Corante*. It came out in London in 1621 and had news from France, Italy, Spain, and other countries in Europe.

When were the first banks opened?

Ever since coins first appeared, some 2,500 years ago, people have traded in money. The word "bank" comes from the Italian *banco*, meaning "bench." In the Middle Ages, moneychangers and merchants did business from benches in the marketplace. The first big national bank was the Bank of England, which was started in 1694. The Federal Reserve, created by an Act of Congress in 1913, acts as a central bank in the United States.

▶ A town crier in the American colonies during the 1600s. A roll on the drum warned people that the crier was about to shout out the latest news.

FIRSTS

■ Canned foods were unknown before the 1800s. They first went on sale in the 1820s.

■ Strangely, the first efficient can opener was not invented until the 1860s, 40 years later! Until then, people opened a can by hitting it with a hammer and chisel.

■ In the 1650s a new craze hit Europe—coffee-drinking. People met in coffee houses to gossip and talk business.

■ The first newspaper with pictures in it was called the *Civic Mercury* and appeared in 1643.

■ The first modern-style refrigerator was invented in 1858, by Ferdinand Carré.

■ The first plastic was invented in the 1860s by an American looking for a substitute for ivory for billiard balls.

◀ The Sumerians, a people of Ancient Mesopotamia, used different clay tokens like these (right) for trading different kinds of goods.

When were postage stamps first used?

By the 1700s most European countries had some sort of postal service. Letters were carried on horseback and by stagecoach.

In 1840 the "penny post" appeared in Britain. Soon countries all over the world were issuing stamps. Stamps made it easier and cheaper for people to send letters.

When were banknotes first used?

Shells, stones, beads, teeth, even cattle, were used as money in ancient times. The first real coins were made from gold and silver. Paper money came later, first in China, and then in Europe during the 1600s.

Sumerian trade tokens

When were labor unions first formed?

The earliest labor unions were probably the trade clubs formed by workers in various trades, such as carpenters and shoemakers, in the 1600s. Labor unions as we know them today grew up when men, women, and children worked in factories created during the Industrial Revolution of the 1800s.

Who pioneered modern nursing?

British soldiers wounded in the Crimean War (1854–1856) called the nurse in charge of their hospital "the lady with the lamp." Today Florence Nightingale is known as the founder of modern nursing.

When was the Red Cross founded?

In 1859, in northern Italy, Austrians and French fought the Battle of Solferino. Men lay wounded in the fierce heat, and among those who saw their suffering was Henri Dunant, a young Swiss banker. Dunant suggested that a society to help wounded soldiers be set up in every country. In 1863 a meeting in Geneva brought the first

▶ Labor unions had banners and paintings made to show what they stood for. The pictures showed workers united to strive for fairness and an improved way of life.

Florence Nightingale

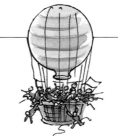

The first use of a balloon in war was in 1794, during the French Revolution, when French observers in a balloon directed cannon fire against Austrian forces.

BE UNITED AND INDUSTRIOUS

AMALGAMATED SOCIETY OF ENGINEERS, MACHINISTS, MILLWRIGHTS, SMITHS, AND PATTERN MAKERS.

Red Cross societies into being. In the United States, Clara Barton helped set up the American Red Cross in 1881. Today the Red Cross is at work all over the world. In Muslim countries, its symbol is a red crescent. Israel uses a red Star of David.

When were planes first used in war?

In 1911 Italy took Libya from Turkey in the Tripolitan War and used planes to drop bombs. In World War I (1914–1918), both sides used airplanes. At first they used them for reconnaissance, but they soon began dropping small bombs and shooting at ground targets. Airplanes were used by armies and navies. Britain formed the first air force, the Royal Air Force, in 1918.

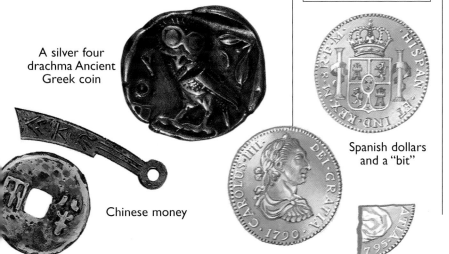

A silver four drachma Ancient Greek coin

Chinese money

Spanish dollars and a "bit"

◀ **Examples of early coins. Chinese money was knife-shaped at first, but most coins are round. Old Spanish dollars were cut into "pieces of eight."**

ARCHITECTURE, PAINTING, AND SCULPTURE

When were columns first used in buildings?

Columns are tall pillars used most often to support the roof of a building. The Ancient Egyptians used columns in their temples and tombs as long ago as 2700 B.C. The columns were of several different styles, with a variety of decorations.

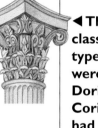

When was the arch first used?

The arch was first used by the people of Mesopotamia 5,000 years ago. They built in brick, and invented forms like the true arch, instead of using great stone horizontal roofing slabs, like the Egyptians. The arch was introduced into Europe by the Etruscans, from about 750 B.C. onward. From them, the Romans learned how to build the arch and developed it even further.

When were the first theaters built?

The first theaters were built by the Ancient Greeks in about the 5th century B.C. We know that the theater of Dionysus in Athens was founded about 500 B.C. It could hold about 18,000 spectators.

▶ The Romans were superb builders. They built large temples, theaters, and forts of stone. They also built bridges and aqueducts with high arches.

◀ The three classical orders, or types, of column were (from left) Doric, Ionic, and Corinthian. Each had a different decoration on its top.

In an Egyptian house, the best place to sleep was on the roof. It was cooler than indoors. The roof was flat, so you couldn't fall off!

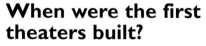

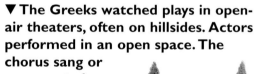

▼ The Greeks watched plays in open-air theaters, often on hillsides. Actors performed in an open space. The chorus sang or commented on the action.

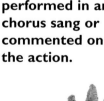

When did buildings first have domes?

Domes were first used in the ancient Near East, the Mediterranean area, and India. At first, they were either solid spherical mounds, or used only on small buildings. The Romans developed domes as roofs in large buildings. One of the earliest examples of a domed building is the Pantheon in Rome. It was built around A.D. 124 for Emperor Hadrian. The vast dome was 142 feet (43.3 m) in diameter and remained the biggest in the world for 1,300 years. The "eye" at the top was left open to let in light and air. To save weight, the walls contained spaces or voids.

▲ **The Pantheon in Rome was made from overlapping concrete rings. The dome got thinner as it rose toward the top.**

▼ **The Parthenon was one of the Greeks' greatest buildings. It stands on a hilltop overlooking Athens.**

What were aqueducts?

The Ancient Romans built tunnels, ditches, and huge bridgelike structures called aqueducts to carry water from rivers and lakes into their cities. Some of these impressive feats of engineering still stand today. A fine example of a Roman aqueduct is the Pont du Gard in France, built about 19 B.C. It is 886 feet (270 m) long.

Where is the Parthenon?

The Parthenon is a beautiful Greek temple that stands on top of the Acropolis, a hilltop site above the city of Athens. The Parthenon was a temple built in honor of the goddess Athena in the 5th century B.C. by order of the Greek leader Pericles. It is one of the most famous ancient buildings in the world.

Who was Christopher Wren?

Christopher Wren (1632–1723) was a British architect who designed St. Paul's Cathedral in London. Wren was given the chance to build the cathedral, and many other new churches in London, after the Great Fire of 1666, which destroyed much of the old medieval city. Work on St. Paul's Cathedral finished in 1710.

When were the first sculptures made?

The earliest sculptures are as much as 30,000 years old, dating from the Stone Age. They are tiny figures representing women, which have come to be known as the "Venuses." Stone Age Venuses have been found all over Europe and western Asia. Stone Age sculptors also made figures of animals.

When were the first watercolors painted?

The use of watercolor in painting has a long history. We know that watercolor paint was used on papyrus rolls in Ancient Egypt, and in the earliest paintings of China.

▲ A terra-cotta (clay) figure of a woman, known as the Venus of Malta. It was made between 3400 and 3000 B.C. and was found on the island of Malta.

When did painters first use perspective?

Perspective is a method of drawing a picture so as to give an impression of realistic depth and distance. The laws of perspective were figured out and first used in the 15th century in Italy. The Italian architect Filippo Brunelleschi (1377–1446) figured out these principles. They are based on the fact that objects seem smaller the closer they are to the horizon.

When did Japanese prints become world-famous?

Japanese color prints in the style known as *ukiyo-e* were first seen in Europe in the late 1800s. They have influenced many European artists since then. *Ukiyo-e* arose in the 16th and 17th centuries to appeal to popular tastes. Some of the works best known in Europe are the landscape prints of Katsushika Hokusai (1760–1849).

Who painted for four years on his back?

One of the greatest artists was Michelangelo, who lived in Italy from 1475 to 1564. He was a painter, a sculptor, and an architect. His greatest painting covers the ceiling of the Sistine Chapel in the Vatican, Rome. It consists of scenes from the Bible— the Creation, the story of Noah and the flood, the apostles—and Michelangelo painted it all by himself, lying flat on his back on scaffolding. It took him four years, from 1508 to 1512.

◀ This fresco, or wall painting, in the Sistine Chapel in Rome is also by Michelangelo. It shows the Day of Judgment.

Which painter tied himself to a ship's mast?

The British painter Joseph Turner, who lived from 1775 to 1851, is renowned for his landscape paintings. His paintings have marvelous effects of color that capture the play of light on a scene—for example, a sunset or a storm. In order to see what a storm at sea really looks like, Turner once had himself tied to the mast of a ship that was sailing through a storm.

Who painted himself for forty years?

Many artists like to paint themselves. The most revealing of all self-portraits are those by the Dutch artist Rembrandt van Rijn, who lived from 1606 to 1669. His portraits capture people's expressions to suggest their inner feelings. Among the best of Rembrandt's portraits are those of himself, which he painted over a period of forty years.

Who were the Impressionists?

The Impressionists were a group of French painters who lived at the end of the 1800s. Instead of painting a scene as it appeared, these artists painted their own impression of it.

▼ A self-portrait of Van Gogh in 1889. His head is bandaged because he cut off his ear during a bout of mental illness. Many artists have painted themselves.

DID YOU KNOW?

■ Among the first artists to paint in oils were the Flemish painters Hubert and Jan Eyck, who lived in the early 1400s.

■ One of the most famous pictures in the world is Leonardo da Vinci's *Mona Lisa*, painted about 1500.

■ In 1905 a group of French painters were called the "wild beasts" because their paintings seemed so violent and distorted. They included Henri Matisse and André Derain.

◄ A portrait by Renoir of two girls, painted about 1895.

► Picasso, here at home in Cannes in 1960, lived a long life and produced an enormous amount of work. He was a painter, sculptor, and graphic artist but also created wonderful pottery.

The paintings have rough outlines and brushstrokes, and are often light in color. In this way, the artists tried to catch the quality of light in a scene. Leading Impressionist painters included Claude Monet, Edouard Manet, Camille Pissarro, Alfred Sisley, and Pierre Auguste Renoir.

Who was Van Gogh?

The Dutch painter Vincent Van Gogh (1853–1890) is famous for his vivid paintings of landscapes, people, and still life. They are painted in broad strokes of strong color. *Sunflowers* has become one of his most popular and famous works. Yet during his lifetime, Van Gogh sold only one painting, and he died a poor man.

Who was Picasso?

Pablo Ruiz y Picasso (1881–1973) was a Spanish artist who must be the best known of all 20th-century painters. He painted in several different styles, and greatly influenced other painters of his day. Picasso spent much of his life in France. He helped develop a style of painting known as Cubism.

LITERATURE AND DRAMA

Who wrote *The Iliad* and *The Odyssey*?

The Iliad and *The Odyssey* are two Greek epic poems that tell the story of the siege of the city of Troy and what happened afterward. Tradition has it that they were written by Homer, a blind singer from the Greek island of Chios. We know very little about Homer—historians are not even sure if both these great poems were made up by one person.

▼ In Homer's *The Odyssey*, Odysseus is tied to the mast so his ship cannot be lured to its doom by the sweet-voiced Sirens.

Who was Virgil?

A famous Roman writer, born in 70 B.C. in Italy. His full name was Publius Vergilius Maro, and his most famous work is *The Aeneid*. This is an epic poem about the fall of Troy and the adventures of a warrior named Aeneas, who leads his followers to Italy, where they were able to settle and found the Roman nation. Virgil also wrote about the work of farmers and the life of the countryside. His writings were read all over Europe during later times, when Latin was a shared language of learning.

▶ The tale of Aladdin and the genie of the lamp is just one of the wonderful stories from *The Thousand and One Nights*.

In ancient times, few people could read. They listened to storytellers and enjoyed tales of gods and goddesses, heroes and monsters.

Who told stories for 1001 nights?

A princess of Arabia named Scheherazade. The story tells how her husband, a cruel king, put to death all his wives. Scheherazade tricked him by telling the king a tale each night, stopping when she got to the most exciting part. If he wanted to hear the rest, he must let her live another day. This went on for 1001 nights, until the king gave up his wicked plan. The stories, traditional and from many parts of Asia, were first written down in Arabic in about A.D. 1000.

Who wrote *The Divine Comedy*?

Dante, an Italian writer born in Florence in 1265. *The Divine Comedy* is one the most important writings of medieval Europe, because Dante wrote in Italian, his own language—

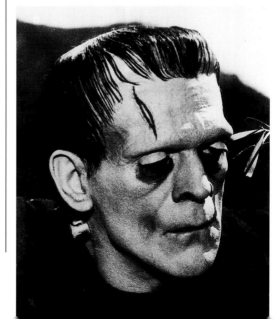

A 19th-century painting of Dante and his "ideal woman," Beatrice. In his great poem *The Divine Comedy*, Dante describes a visit to Heaven with Beatrice.

Was there a real Robinson Crusoe?

The tale of Robinson Crusoe, a shipwrecked sailor, was written by the English journalist Daniel Defoe (1660–1731) in 1719. It has remained popular ever since. Defoe got the idea from real-life tales of the sea, and sailors—in particular the story of Alexander Selkirk, a well-known survivor of a shipwreck. To make this story more believable, Defoe put in lots of detail about Crusoe's adventures.

Who created Frankenstein's monster?

English author Mary Shelley (1797–1851), the wife of poet Percy Bysshe Shelley (1792–1822). Her story of the scientist Frankenstein, and the monster he made out of humans, was published in 1818. In it, the monster finally destroys the scientist.

▼ Frankenstein's monster, created by Mary Shelley, has appeared in many movies and on TV.

and not in Latin, which was then the language of education and scholarship. It is a poem in three parts describing journeys through Hell, Purgatory, and finally Heaven.

What are *The Canterbury Tales*?

A collection of stories in verse, supposed to have been told by pilgrims on their way from London to Canterbury in the 1300s. The stories were written by the English poet Geoffrey Chaucer (1342–1400). They reflect the characters and lives of the tellers.

> ### DID YOU KNOW?
>
> ■ A famous woman poet of the ancient world was Sappho. She lived on an island in the Aegean Sea between 610 and 580 B.C.
>
> ■ Fables (short stories with a moral) are a traditional favorite.
>
> ■ Many fables are supposed to have been told by a Greek slave named Aesop. But Aesop was probably not a real person at all.
>
> ■ Fairy tales are very old. The first collections of European fairy tales were made in 1697 by the French writer Charles Perrault.
>
> ■ A great Indian epic poem, *The Ramayana*, tells of the adventures of a king named Rama. It was written about 300 B.C.
>
> ■ The first important novel was *The Tale of Genji*, written by a court lady in Japan about 1010.

◄ Chaucer's pilgrims told stories on the way from London to Canterbury. This picture shows several pilgrims on the road.

Who was Moby Dick?

Moby Dick was a great white whale, whose story was written by the novelist Herman Melville (1819–1891). It is a thrilling story of whaling in the 19th century, but with deeper, more symbolic meanings as well. Melville had been to sea on whaling ships and seen many adventures, including being shipwrecked and taking part in a spectacular mutiny.

Hans Andersen told the story of a Chinese emperor who loved a nightingale's song. When the bird flew away, he had a mechanical bird made in its place.

FAMOUS BOOKS

■ In *Gulliver's Travels*, by Jonathan Swift (1667–1745), Gulliver has strange adventures among giants, minuscule people, and talking horses.

■ The French writer Alexandre Dumas (1803–1870) wrote the exciting adventures of *The Three Musketeers*.

■ The first detective stories were written by Edgar Allan Poe (1809–1849).

■ English novelist Charlotte Brontë (1816–1854) wrote *Jane Eyre*. Her sister Emily (1818–1849) wrote *Wuthering Heights*.

■ Lewis Carroll's real name was Charles Lutwidge Dodgson (1832–1898). He wrote *Alice's Adventures in Wonderland*.

Who was Hans Christian Andersen?

A Danish writer of children's stories, such as *The Ugly Duckling* and *The Little Mermaid*. Hans Andersen was born in 1805 and died in 1875. His stories were based on traditional tales, but were different from those collected by the Brothers Grimm. Instead of being about giants and witches, many of Andersen's stories are gentle and reflect his own sad and lonely life.

Why is Charles Dickens so popular?

Many readers think Charles Dickens was the greatest of all English novelists. His books include such favorites as *Pickwick Papers, A Christmas Carol*, and *Oliver Twist*. Dickens was born in 1812. His early life was spent in poverty, and he used these harsh experiences in his novels.

▲ The hunchback of Notre Dame became the star of a Disney cartoon movie—which would have surprised his French creator, Victor Hugo!

Who created *The Hunchback of Notre Dame*?

French writer Victor Hugo (1802–1885) was a poet, playwright, and novelist. His most famous novels are *The Hunchback of Notre Dame* and *Les Misérables*, a story about an escaped convict who tries to lead an honest life. For his political views, Hugo was banished from France for a time.

▶ The jovial Mr. Pickwick, from Charles Dickens's *Pickwick Papers*, celebrates one of his many adventures.

Who wrote the first science fiction stories?

Jules Verne (1828–1905), a French writer. In his imagination, he foresaw journeys into space by rocket, the development of the submarine, and the invention of television.

Who was Mark Twain?

A writer whose real name was Samuel Langhorne Clemens. He lived from 1835 to 1910, and his best-known books are *The Adventures of Tom Sawyer* and *The Adventures of Huckleberry Finn*. He took his pen name, which means "Mark Two," from the call of the riverboatmen as they measured the depth of water along the Mississippi River.

Who wrote the first tragedies?

Tragedy is a kind of drama that grew up in Ancient Greece. Writers of Greek tragedy included Aeschylus (525–456 B.C.), Sophocles (496–406 B.C.), and Euripides (484–406 B.C.). In Greek plays, the actors were joined on the open-air stage by a chorus. The chorus sang and commented on the action of the play. Early Greek plays had unhappy endings, but later Euripides began writing plays with happy endings, starting a new trend in Greek drama.

Who was England's greatest dramatist?

England's greatest dramatist was also the world's greatest. He was William Shakespeare (1564–1616). He was born in Stratford-upon-Avon but went to London, where he became

◀ Mark Twain's real name was Samuel Clemens. He once worked as a riverboat captain, and "mark twain" was the call for water two fathoms deep.

▼ Shakespeare's plays were staged in London's lively open-air theaters, such as the Globe. All the actors were men, even those playing female roles.

involved in the theater, as an actor and as a writer and director. His plays cover a wide range of subjects and include histories, comedies such as *A Midsummer Night's Dream,* and tragedies such as *Hamlet.* They are performed all over the world.

Who was Anton Chekhov?

Chekhov was a Russian playwright and writer of short stories. Among his best-known plays are *Uncle Vanya* and *The Seagull.* He wrote about the decline of the landowning class in Russia. Chekhov was born in 1860 and trained as a doctor. He died in 1904.

MUSIC AND DANCE

When were musical instruments first played?

Musical instruments have been played since prehistoric times. The earliest instruments were objects such as seashells and bone pipes. Music accompanied dancing and religious ceremonies. People of the ancient civilizations of Mesopotamia, Egypt, India, China, and Greece then started to listen to music purely for enjoyment and pleasure.

When did the modern orchestra first appear?

The first orchestras appeared at the beginning of the 1600s, as part of Italian opera. They included nearly all the instruments known at that time, except drums. In the 1700s, composers in Germany began to write music for four groups of instruments in the orchestra— woodwind (such as flutes and oboes), brass (horns and trumpets), percussion (drums), and strings (violins, cellos, and basses)—the basis of the orchestra.

When was music first written down?

In Ancient Egypt, Mesopotamia, and Greece. Experts believe they have found written music from Sumeria, a hymn dating from between 5,000 and 3,000 years ago. The first written music that survives complete dates from the A.D. 800s.

▲ A 17th-century orchestra. The musicians are playing string and brass instruments and an organ.

Singers sound better in the bath! The sounds of your voice bounce off the walls and the water to make rich, loud echoes.

▶ A song written down in the Middle Ages. Musical notes are written on the stave (the lines) with the words underneath.

When was opera first performed?

Around 1600 in Italy, stage plays were set to music. The first-known stage play set to music was produced in 1597, but its music has not survived. The first two surviving operas were performed in 1600. Claudio Monteverdi (1567–1643) was the first great opera composer. His opera *Orfeo* was first performed in 1607.

When was ballet first staged?

Ballet as we know it developed in the 1800s, from earlier forms of court and stage dances. France's King Louis XIV founded a royal school of dancing in 1661. In the late 1800s and early 1900s, Russian ballet became the most famous in the world.

Who was Pavlova?

Anna Pavlova was a famous Russian ballet dancer. She was famous for her solo performances, especially "The Dying Swan." Pavlova was born in St. Petersburg in Russia in 1882 and toured with the famous Ballets Russes company formed by Sergei Diaghilev (1872–1929). She died in 1931.

Who was Johann Sebastian Bach?

Bach (1685–1750) was a German composer. His family were all musicians. Bach was trained as a church organist and wrote a lot of church music. While working as musical director to a German prince, he wrote some of his best-loved music—the *Brandenburg Concertos*. Another great work by Bach is his *St. Matthew Passion*.

▶ The young Mozart astonished everyone with his brilliance as a musician. He grew up to be one of the greatest of all composers.

◀ Pavlova danced "The Dying Swan" so movingly that she held audiences spellbound.

▼ Johann Sebastian Bach is shown here at the keyboard, with some of his many children and his second wife, Anna Magdalena.

When did Mozart start composing music?

When he was only five! Wolfgang Amadeus Mozart (1756–1791) was an Austrian musical genius. As a child prodigy, he toured Europe showing his skill on the harpsichord and violin. He wrote concertos, symphonies, and several great operas including *The Marriage of Figaro*, *The Magic Flute*, and *Don Giovanni*. Despite his brilliant talent, he earned little money and died a pauper. In 30 years he had written more then 600 works.

Which famous composer could not hear his own music?

Ludwig van Beethoven (1770–1827) was one of the greatest composers—yet he was deaf for much of his life. Beethoven was born in Germany, and studied music under Joseph Haydn (1732–1809). He began to lose his hearing at the age of 32, but went on writing music because he could hear the sounds in his head. His many great works include nine symphonies and the *Emperor Concerto*.

▲ Elvis Presley's recordings were hits all over the world. He also starred in a number of films.

Who was Elvis Presley?

Elvis Presley was one of the first superstars of rock music. He became popular in the 1950s and 1960s with songs such as *Heartbreak Hotel* and *Jailhouse Rock*. He also recorded love songs and traditional songs. Presley was born in 1935 in Tennessee. He died in 1977, but his music continues to sell.

When was Beatle-mania?

The Beatles were a music group from Liverpool, England who became famous in the 1960s when "Beatle-mania" was at its height. The four Beatles were John Lennon (1940–1980), Paul McCartney (born 1942), George Harrison (born 1943), and Ringo Starr (real name Richard Starkey, born 1940). The Beatles split up in 1970 to follow solo careers. John Lennon was shot dead in New York City in 1980.

▼ Beatles fans outside Buckingham Palace try to see their idols, who were receiving an award from the Queen.

▲ King Oliver's Creole Jazz Band, in about 1920. The kneeling player at the front is Louis Armstrong.

When was jazz first played?

The style of music known as jazz began in the southern states of the United States, but had its roots in traditional African and American folk music, including religious songs known as spirituals. The home of jazz is New Orleans in Louisiana, where black musicians formed jazz bands in the early 1900s.

Music isn't always written down. Jazz musicians often make up the music as they go along. This is called a "jam session."

SPORTS

◀ In a Roman chariot race, the drivers drove four-horse teams around a track called a hippodrome. Watching crowds placed bets on the results.

Where did people race chariots?

In ancient times, chariot races were popular in Egypt and Rome. In Rome, chariots pulled by horses raced around oval-shaped tracks. Spectators often got very excited, so much so that supporters of the losers sometimes started riots.

▼ Knights jousting in the Middle Ages tried to knock one another out of the saddle with their lances.

People have raced all sorts and sizes of animals. There have been ostrich races and snail races!

What sports did people enjoy in the Middle Ages?

Hunting, with dogs and trained hawks, was a popular recreation for nobles. Knights practiced their fighting skills in mock-fights called jousts. Archery, shooting with bows and arrows, was also popular.

Where would you see Sumo wrestling?

In Japan. Sumo wrestlers are mostly very fat men. This form of wrestling dates from 1624 and is still very popular in Japan.

How old is skiing?

People were using skis to travel over snow thousands of years ago. Modern skiing dates from the mid-1800s.

How old is skateboarding?

Skateboarding began in California in the 1930s. Surfing enthusiasts built boards with wheels to try out surfing techniques on dry land. Modern boards are made of fiberglass, metal, plastic, or wood. Experts can perform daredevil tricks on their boards.

Who invented baseball?

Some baseball fans credit Abner Doubleday (1819–1893) as the inventor of modern baseball in 1839. Official rules were drawn up in 1845. Baseball is so popular in the United States that it is often referred to as the "national pastime."

▼ A baseball player swings the bat to make a hit.

Where was basketball first played?

Basketball was invented in 1891 by a Canadian named James Naismith, a teacher in Massachusetts. He was asked to create a team sport that college students could play indoors during the winter. At first, soccer balls were used.

◀ In basketball, players leap to lob or drop the ball into the basket. Tall players have an advantage.

◀ Skateboarders wear pads to protect their knees and elbows as they whizz around.

▼ In the Middle Ages people played a rough kind of football with few rules. In 1314 the English king banned football because it was so rowdy.

When did people first play football?

In the 1300s football was a game in which crowds brawled over a ball. It was thought an "undignified and worthless" game. Rules for soccer and American football were drawn up in the 1800s, when college students and working men took up team games with great enthusiasm. This led to the growth of professional teams.

▲ **Rugby players leap for the ball at a lineout. In this game, there are 15 players on each team.**

Who first played rugby?

In 1823 a boy at Rugby School in England ignored the rules of soccer and picked up the ball in his arms and ran with it. This was the beginning of a new game, named after the school, in which the ball is handled as well as kicked.

How did gymnastics become a modern sport?

Gymnastics in the form of tumbling and acrobatics has been around since earliest times. In the late 1800s German schools started to teach organized gymnastics as part of physical fitness programs. Gymnastics has been an Olympic sport since the modern Olympic Games began in 1896. There are exercises for men and women, for which points are scored.

SPORTS FACTS

■ There are pictures of archers in Stone Age cave paintings.

■ The first modern Olympic Games were held at Athens, Greece, in 1896.

■ The fastest ball game is pelota, in which the ball travels at about 186 mph (300 km/h).

■ The first horse jumping competition in modern times was staged in London in 1869.

■ The Dutch played ice hockey in the 1500s, but modern ice hockey began in Canada in the 1850s.

■ The Romans had rowing races, but boat races were probably held even earlier.

■ The first country to stage formally organized swimming races was Japan, in about 35 B.C.

▼ **Fast-moving Muhammad Ali is probably the most famous boxer of all time. He predicted the outcome of his fights in rhyme.**

What was prizefighting?

Fist-fighting for money. Boxing is one of the oldest sports, dating from Greek and Roman times. In London, during the 1700s men known as prizefighters fought in a ring, and spectators bet on the result. The fighters wore no gloves, and bouts went on for many rounds until one man could not continue.

Who played bowls before a battle?

For a time in the 1300s bowls was banned in England because the king feared people would lose interest in archery. But the game remained popular. Sir Francis Drake (1540?–1596) is said to have played bowls while waiting to sail into battle against the Spanish Armada in 1588.

Who is Muhammad Ali?

Muhammad Ali (Cassius Clay) became the first boxer to hold the world heavyweight title three times (1964–67, 1974–78, 1978–79). He was born in 1942 in Kentucky. He was stripped of his world title in 1967 after refusing to fight in the Vietnam War on religious grounds.

When were the Olympic Games first held in the United States?

In 1904, when the third modern Olympics were staged at St. Louis. The Games returned to the United States in 1932 (Los Angeles), 1984 (Los Angeles again), and 1996 (Atlanta).

When was the first soccer World Cup competition?

In 1930. Uruguay was the winner, beating Argentina 4–2 in the final. In 1994 the United States hosted the finals, and Brazil won the cup for a record fourth time.

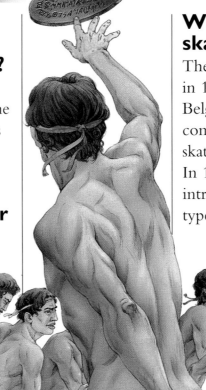

When were the first auto races?

Organized auto racing started in France in 1895, when the Automobile Club de France staged a race between Paris and Bordeaux. Twenty-two drivers started the race but only nine finished. Also in 1895, a pioneer auto race was run in Chicago. It was won by J. Frank Duryea.

When was the first Indianapolis 500?

This famous auto race was first held in 1911 in the United States. Winning speeds are now more than twice as fast as the winning car in the 1911 race—74 mph (120 km/h). The race is held on the 2½-mile (4.02 km) Indianapolis Motor Speedway. Drivers race to complete 200 laps of the track.

▲ The Greek athletes who took part in the ancient Olympic Games wore no clothes. Running and throwing the discus were two of the events in the ancient Games.

Lacrosse was first played by the Iroquois of North America. There might be as many as 1,000 people in each team! Games lasted hours.

When were roller skates invented?

The first roller skates were invented in 1760 by Joseph Merlin, of Huy, Belgium. He is supposed to have come sailing into a ballroom on his skates, playing a violin, and crashed. In 1863, James Plimpton of New York introduced the modern four-wheeled type of roller skate.

Which modern game was first played by Native Americans?

When French explorers reached Canada in the 1500s, they found the Iroquois playing the game that we now call lacrosse. This name comes from the French words *la crosse*, meaning "the crutch." The crosse, or stick, is a bit like a hook with a strong net stretched across it to carry the ball.

How did the marathon race get its name?

It takes its name from the town of Marathon in Greece. It celebrates the run of a messenger named Pheidippides who, in 490 B.C., ran from Marathon to Athens, carrying news of an Athenian victory in battle over the Persians. The distance from Marathon to Athens is about 24¾ miles (40 km), but the modern marathon is more than 26 miles (42 km). The race is held around city roads, not on an arena track, so each course is different.

MYTHS, LEGENDS, AND HEROES

Who was Hercules?

Heracles (called Hercules by the Romans) was the most popular hero of the ancient world. Above all, he was famous for his strength. Hercules performed 12 labors, or tasks. The king who set these challenges thought no man could carry them out. But Hercules completed each task. He fought wild animals and many-headed monsters; captured man-eating horses and shot man-eating birds. He cleaned out the stables of 3,000 beasts by changing the course of a river. He carried the world on his shoulders and also went into the Underworld, the world of the dead.

Who was Helen of Troy?

The Greeks called her the most beautiful woman in the world. Her name was Helen and she was the daughter of Zeus, king of the gods. Her beauty led to the war between Greece and Troy. Helen was carried off by Paris, prince of Troy. Her husband Menelaus sought vengeance, and with his brother Agamemnon led an army of Greeks against Troy. The war lasted ten years.

▼ Athena was the guardian-goddess of Athens. She was loved and feared, and people came to her temple with gifts of food and drink which they dutifully offered up to the huge statue of Athena.

Which goddess gave her name to a great city?

The Ancient Greek city of Athens grew up around a hill called the Acropolis. On it was built a temple to house the city's own guardian goddess, Athena. Athena was a favorite child of Zeus, father of the gods of Ancient Greece. According to legend, she sprang full-grown from her father's head—after he had swallowed her mother.

Who lived at Camelot?

In the Middle Ages, storytellers loved to recount the deeds of brave knights. None were braver or more chivalrous than King Arthur and his Knights of the Round Table, who rode forth from their castle at Camelot. If there was a real-life Camelot, it was probably a fortress in western Britain. The real King Arthur may have lived around A.D. 500, fighting foreign invaders.

Roman soldiers "borrowed" gods from the countries they conquered. They hoped the various gods would protect them from fierce enemies!

Who was Roland?

A French poem written about 1100 tells the story of Roland, one of the noblest knights to serve Charlemagne, king of the Franks. The real Roland was Prefect of Brittany and fought with Charlemagne's army against the Arabs in Spain. In 778 the victorious troops marched home to France. But an ambush lay in wait in the mountains. The rear guard, including Roland, were all killed.

Who was El Cid?

The national hero of Spain is Rodrigo Diaz de Vivar, better known by the title "El Cid Campeador"—the Lord Champion. El Cid was born in Spain about 1040. At this time Spain was divided between the Moors (Arabs) and Spanish rulers. He became a mercenary, or "soldier of fortune," leading his own men to take up arms for any who needed his help. Sometimes he fought for the Moors and sometimes for the Spanish. He was never defeated and ruled the kingdom of Valencia from 1094 until his death in 1099.

Who was William Tell?

The tale of William Tell, Switzerland's national hero, is legendary. But about 1300 there may have been a man who helped to free the Swiss from Austrian rule. The tale tells how the Austrian governor Gessler ordered all the Swiss in Altdorf to bow to a hat set up on a pole in the market square. Tell refused and was arrested. Gessler offered Tell his freedom—if he could shoot an apple from his son's head with an arrow. Tell did so.

FAMOUS DATES

- 4 B.C. Birth of Jesus Christ.
- 43 A.D. Roman conquest of Britain begins.
- 476 Fall of the western Roman Empire.
- 570 Prophet Muhammad born at Mecca.
- 1492 Columbus sails to the New World.
- 1588 English defeat Spanish Armada.
- 1620 Pilgrim Fathers sail to North America.
- 1666 Great Fire of London.
- 1776 American colonists declare independence.
- 1789 French Revolution begins.
- 1865 End of Civil War.
- 1914–1918 World War I.
- 1917 Russian Revolution.
- 1939–1945 World War II.
- 1969 First people land on the Moon.

Who was Prester John?

At the time of the Crusades, tales were told in Europe of a Christian land in the East, ruled by the priest-king Prester John. Later stories placed the legendary kingdom in Africa. Prester John lived only in legend. In 1154 he was described as a powerful leader, ready to help in the Crusaders' fight for the Holy Land. His own kingdom was said to lie beyond Persia, now called Iran.

Who were Anne Bonny and Mary Read?

The waters of the Caribbean were favorite haunts for pirates in the 1600s and 1700s. There were few women pirates on the high seas. Anne Bonny and Mary Read, however, were just as tough as their male shipmates. Both women ran away to sail with the pirate captain John Rackham. Mary Read was captured and died of fever in prison. Anne Bonny was also caught, but her fate thereafter is not known.

◀ The pirates Anne Bonny and Mary Read were unusual in being women. Most pirates were men, such as "Calico" Jack Rackham.

Who was Admiral Nelson?

Nelson was a British naval hero. Born in 1753, he joined the Navy when only 12. He lost his right arm and the sight of his right eye in battle. In 1798 he defeated the French fleet at the Battle of the Nile, and in 1801 won another victory at Copenhagen in Denmark. Nelson became a national hero. He was made a viscount, and carried on a famous love affair with Lady Hamilton, the wife of a diplomat. In 1805 he led the British fleet to victory against the French and Spanish at the battle of Trafalgar. During the battle, Nelson was shot on the deck of his flagship, *Victory*, and he died soon afterward.

Who was Hiawatha?

There are many stories about Hiawatha, but known facts about his life are few. He was a Mohawk, living in the northwestern part of what is now the United States. Around 1575 he persuaded the various tribes to forget their differences and join together in the Iroquois League. The tribes held onto their land against white settlers for 200 years.

▲ At the Battle of Trafalgar in 1805, Admiral Nelson commanded the British fleet. Walking on deck in his admiral's uniform and medals, he was spotted and shot by an enemy sniper.

▼ Hiawatha persuaded the other Iroquois tribes to join his Mohawks against their enemies, the Algonquins.

Who was Pocahontas?

Pocahontas (1595–1617) lived in Virginia, at the time when the first English settlers were arriving in North America. Her tribe captured a settler leader named Captain John Smith. Just as the captive was about to be put to death, Pocahontas rushed forward and begged her father, the chief, to spare him. She later married a settler named John Rolfe, and in 1616 he took her to England. There she met the king and queen. Pocahontas died just before she was due to sail back to Virginia.

Who was Geronimo?

Geronimo's people, the Chiricahua Apache, lived in Arizona in the Southwest. His real name was Gogathlay, or "One Who Yawns," and he was born in 1829. Geronimo fought the Mexicans and the Americans to defend the Apaches' hunting grounds. In 1874 the U.S. Army moved the Apaches to a barren reservation, but Geronimo and a small band of warriors continued to fight. He eluded the army until 1886.

▲ Geronimo

Was Calamity Jane a real person?

Calamity Jane was not her real name. She was born Martha Canary (also known as Martha Burk), probably in 1852. She lived in Deadwood, South Dakota, which at that time was a rip-roaring western frontier town. She could ride and shoot, and her real-life adventures were exaggerated in novels. When Calamity Jane died in 1903, the exciting days of the Wild West were coming to an end.

Who was Spartacus?

In the Roman Empire, slaves did most of the work. Some slaves were treated well, but many were not. In 71 B.C. there was a slaves' revolt, led by a gladiator named Spartacus. The slaves hoped to escape to their native lands, but after two years they were finally defeated. Spartacus was one of the many who died in battle.

▲ While held captive by Native Americans, Daniel Boone was forced to "run the gauntlet." He had to run between two rows of warriors armed with clubs.

▼ A scene from the film *Spartacus*, showing the gladiator leading his slave army in battle.

Who was Daniel Boone?

In the 1700s white settlers began moving westward across America. One of the first frontiersmen was the hunter and trapper Daniel Boone (1734–1820). Like other frontiersmen, Daniel Boone lived by hunting and trapping wild animals. But he also founded settlements; one was called Boonesborough after him. His own wife and daughter were the first white women to live in Kentucky.

Who was Ned Kelly?

In Australia, during the 1800s, outlaws were known as "bushrangers." Ned Kelly was the last, and most famous, of the bushrangers. He was born in 1855 and formed a gang with his brother, raiding rich landowners and stealing horses. The gang's daring robberies made them famous, and some poorer farmers admired Ned Kelly as a kind of Australian Robin Hood. In the end, Kelly's luck ran out. His gang was caught by troopers at a township called Glenrowan. All the outlaws were shot dead, except Ned Kelly, who was wearing homemade armor for protection. He was wounded and captured. Kelly was tried and executed in 1880.

Who was Davy Crockett?

Davy Crockett was born in Tennessee in 1786. He had little formal schooling, spending much of his time in the mountains, hunting bears and fighting Native Americans. Then he became a politician and was elected to Congress. In 1835, defeated in an election, he headed for Texas to help the Texans in their fight for independence (Texas was then ruled by Mexico). In 1836 Davy Crockett was one of two hundred defenders of the Alamo mission, fighting off a Mexican army. In one of the most famous battles in U.S. history all the defenders were killed.

Was there a real Robin Hood?

For over 600 years stories have been told of the English outlaw Robin Hood, who "robbed the rich to help the poor." The real Robin Hood may have been a Saxon, who lost his land following the Norman conquest of

◄ **A portrait of Davy Crockett, whose fame as a frontiersman helped take him to Congress.**

▶ **Robin Hood, pictured here with two of his outlaw companions, Friar Tuck and Little John.**

DID YOU KNOW?

■ A Pawnee adopted Daniel Boone as his son.

■ Geronimo lived in Oklahoma after his surrender. He died in 1908.

■ Several places in northern England are named after Robin Hood.

■ Jesse James's brother, Frank, was tried but freed. He spent the rest of his life as a farmer.

■ Spartacus was born in what is now Bulgaria.

▲ **Jesse James became a folk hero in the South, despite his crimes.**

England in 1066. Some stories tell of him living in Sherwood Forest, Nottinghamshire, at the time of King Richard I (1157–1199). So two, or more, real outlaws may lie behind the legend.

Who was Jesse James?

One of the most famous outlaws of the Wild West. Jesse James was from Missouri, and fought for the South during the Civil War. When the South was defeated at the end of the war, Jesse and his brother Frank turned to crime. They robbed banks and railroads. Eventually, a large reward was offered for Jesse's capture, dead or alive. In 1882 he was shot dead by Robert Ford, one of his own gang, who claimed the reward.

Who was Amelia Earhart?

Amelia Earhart was the first woman to cross the Atlantic Ocean by plane in 1928 as a passenger. Then in 1932, she made the first-ever solo Atlantic flight by a woman. In 1937, Amelia Earhart disappeared while flying across the Pacific Ocean.

HISTORY QUIZ

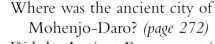

INDEX